Florid and Unusual Alphabets

by
Midolle,
Silvestre
and Others

Dover Publications, Inc., New York

Published in Canada by General Publishing Company, Ltd.,
30 Lesmill Road, Don Mills, Toronto, Ontario.
Published in the United Kingdom by Constable and
Company, Ltd.

Florid and Unusual Alphabets, first published by Dover
Publications, Inc., in 1976, is a new selection of alphabets
from the four works listed in the Publisher's Note on the
opposite page. The Publisher's Note has been written specially
for the present volume.

DOVER *Pictorial Archive* SERIES

Manufactured in the United States of America
Dover Publications, Inc.
31 East 2nd Street
Mineola, N.Y. 11501

Publisher's Note

The nineteenth century was a fertile era both in the invention of striking new alphabets and in the rediscovery of great alphabets of earlier periods. From four of the most famous and sumptuous albums devoted to this material, we have chosen 109 complete alphabets of a highly decorative or unusual nature, of which 33 are lower-case. The sequence we have adopted is, in general, from florid Roman alphabets, to eccentric Roman alphabets, to alphabets partaking of both Roman and Gothic (black-letter) features, to strictly Gothic alphabets.

It should be recalled that in many older and foreign alphabets, one character does duty for both I and J, one character for both U and V, and that certain letters (for instance, W) may not be present.

The alphabets are reproduced from the following works (the page numbers are those of the present volume):

Alphabet-Album / Collection de Soixante Feuilles d'Alphabets Historiés et Fleuronnés Tirés des principales Bibliothèques de l'Europe, ou Composés par Silvestre Professeur de Calligraphie des Princes. Gravés par Girault / Paris / 1843 / Chez J. Techener, Editeur, Place du Louvre, No. 12: pages 1, 2, 4, 5, 8, 9, 10, 11, 15, 28, 30, 32, 33, 34, 35, 36, 37, 38, 44, 45, 46, 49, 50, 51, 52, 53, 58, 59, 62, 64, 65, 66, 67, 69, 71, 73, 74, 75, 78.

Bellezas de la caligrafía por R. Stirling. Comendador de la Real Órden americana de Isabel la Católica. Tercera [3rd] edicion. Barcelona. Librería de Joaquín Verdaguer. Rambla núm. 5, frente al Liceo; n.d. [c. 1844]: pages 3, 6, 7, 12, 31, 39.

Zierschriften von Karl Klimsch. Band [Volume] I. Lithographische Anstalt & Verlag Klimsch & Co., Frankfurt a/M; n.d.: pages 14, 16, 17, 18, 19, 20, 21, 22, 23, 24, 25, 26, 27, 40, 41, 54, 55, 56, 57, 63, 70, 79, 80, 81, 82, 83, 84, 85, 86, 87, 88, 89.

Galerie. Compositions avec Ecritures Anciennes et Modernes exécutées à la Plume par J. Midolle Artiste Ecrivain Compositeur et Membre de plusieurs Sociétés d'Arts. Gravées et publiées à la Lithographie de E. Simon Fils à Strasbourg 1834/1835: pages 13, 29, 42, 43, 47, 48, 60, 61, 68, 72, 76, 77.

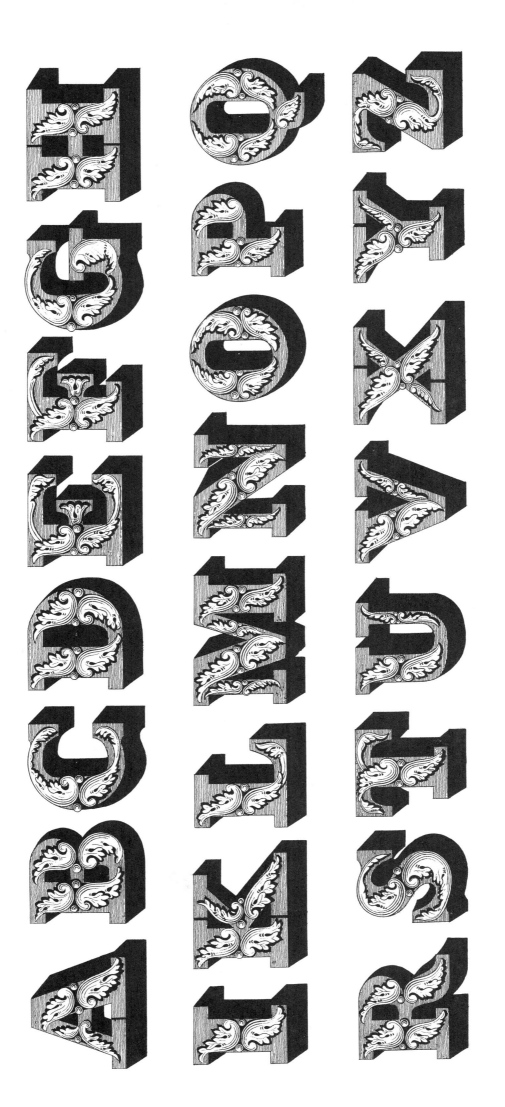

1 Silvestre: "19th Century; Foliated Capitals"

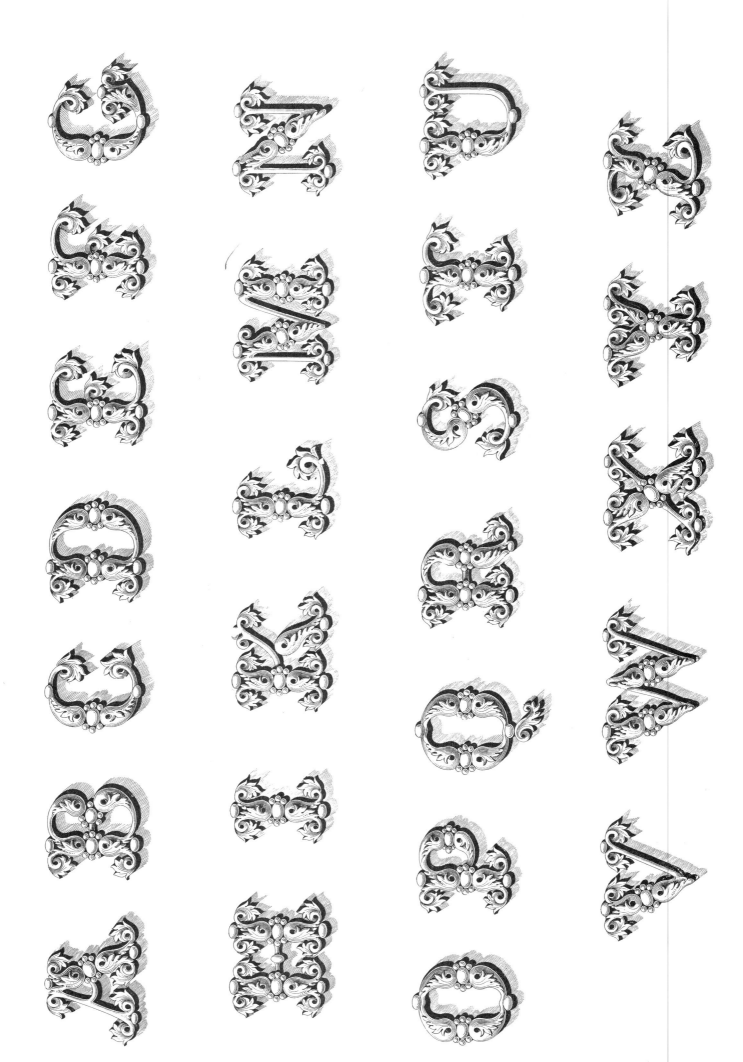

2   Silvestre: "19th Century; French; Foliated Capitals"

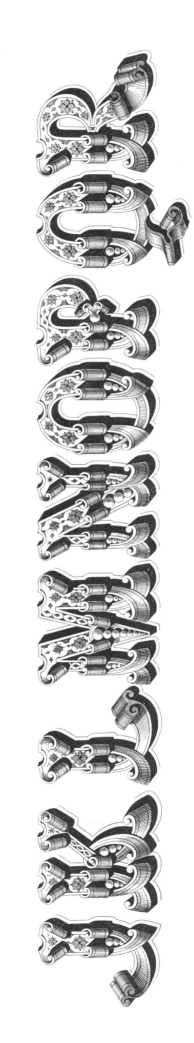
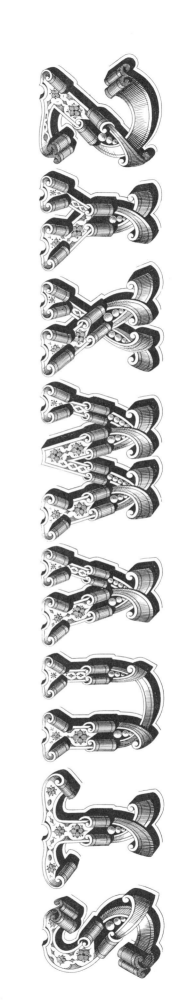

4   Silvestre: "Composite Capitals (Midolle)"

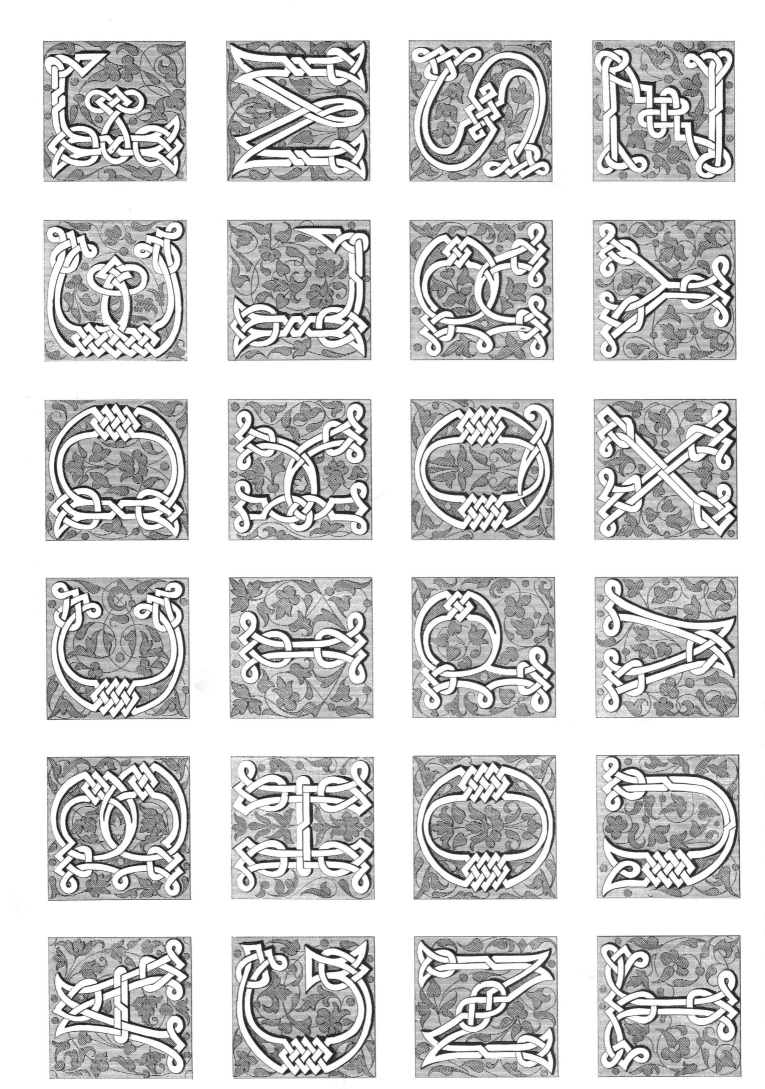

5   Silvestre: "19th Century; Imitation of Saxon Letters"

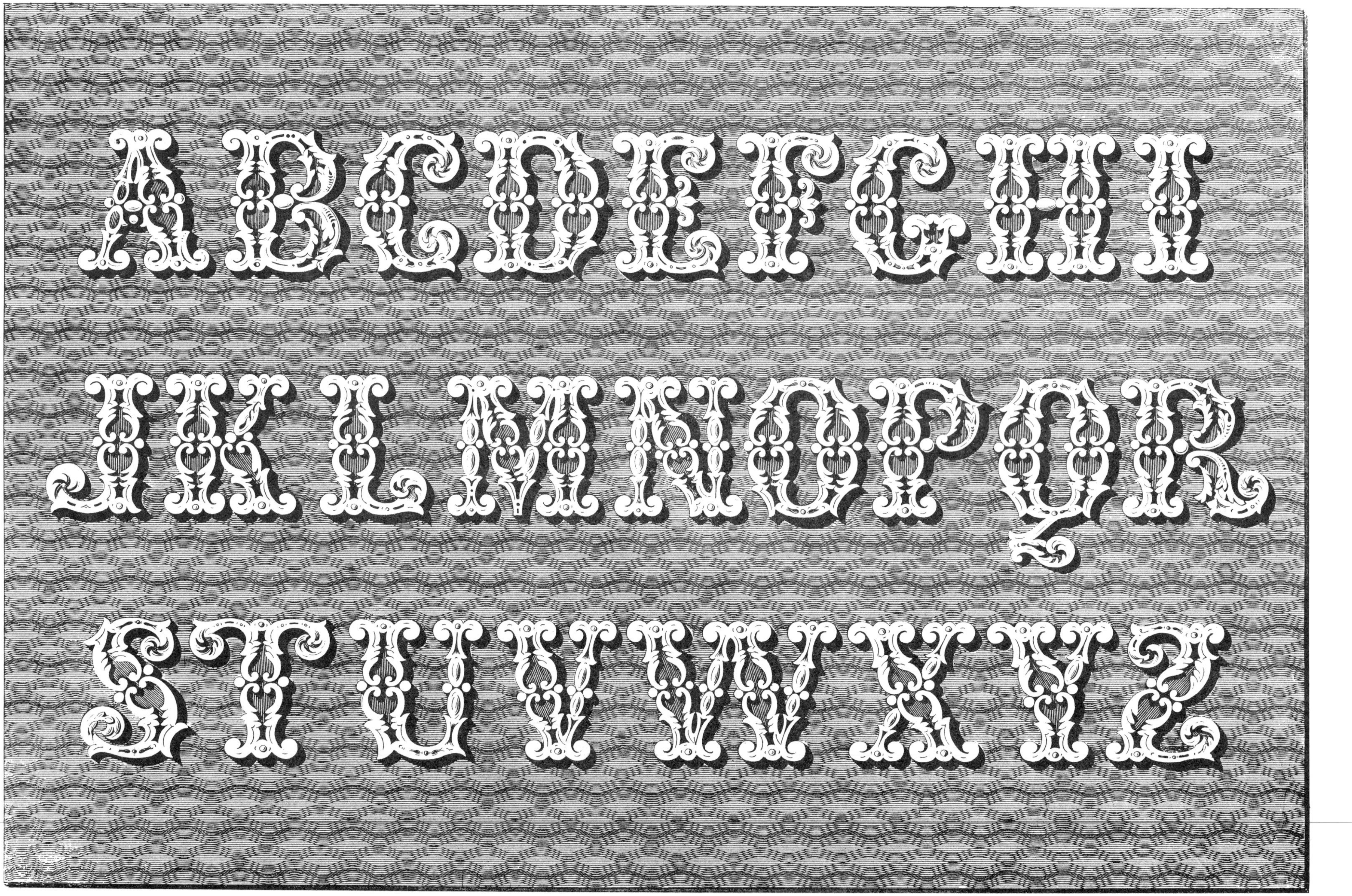

 Stirling

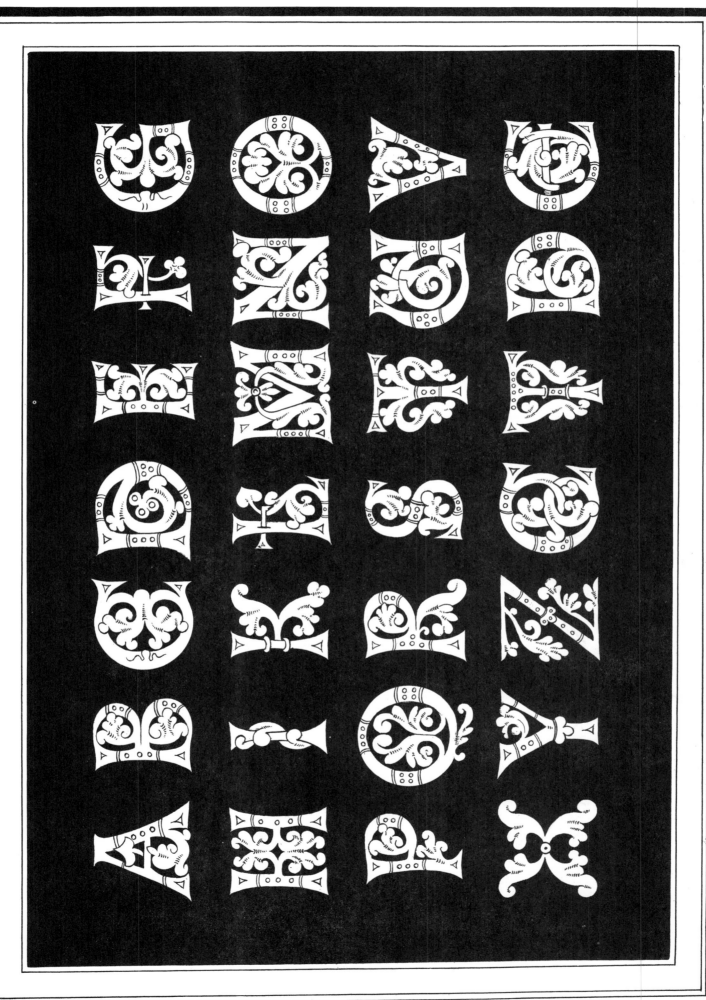

9   Silvestre: "13th Century; Italian; from Financial Secretary Fouquet's Bible, Paris Royal Library"

10   Silvestre: "17th Century; Italian; from a MS in the Library of St. Mark's, Venice"

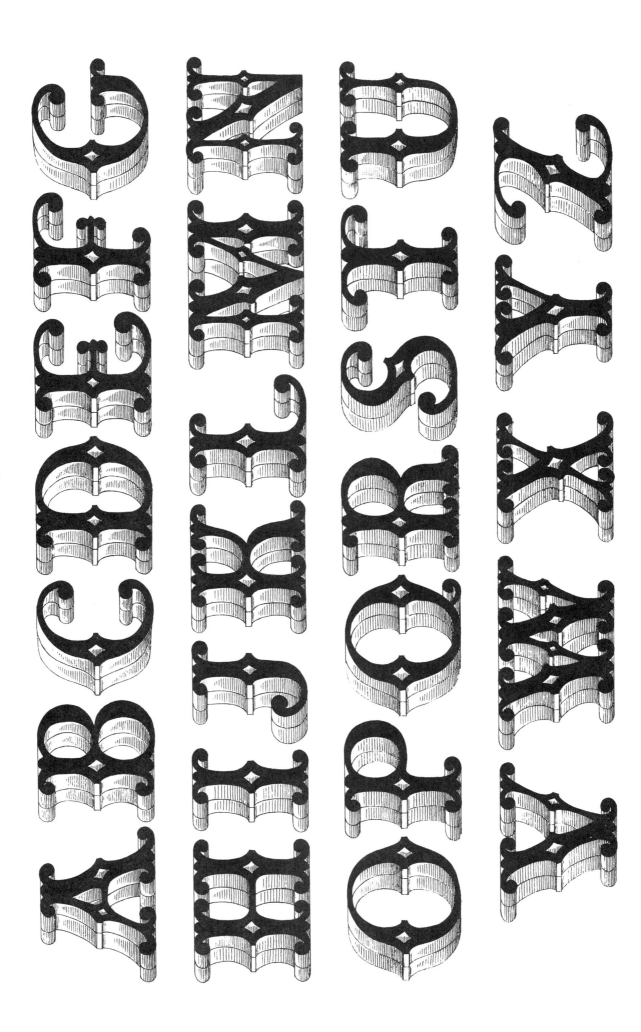

11 Silvestre: "19th Century; Three-Dimensional Roman Capitals"

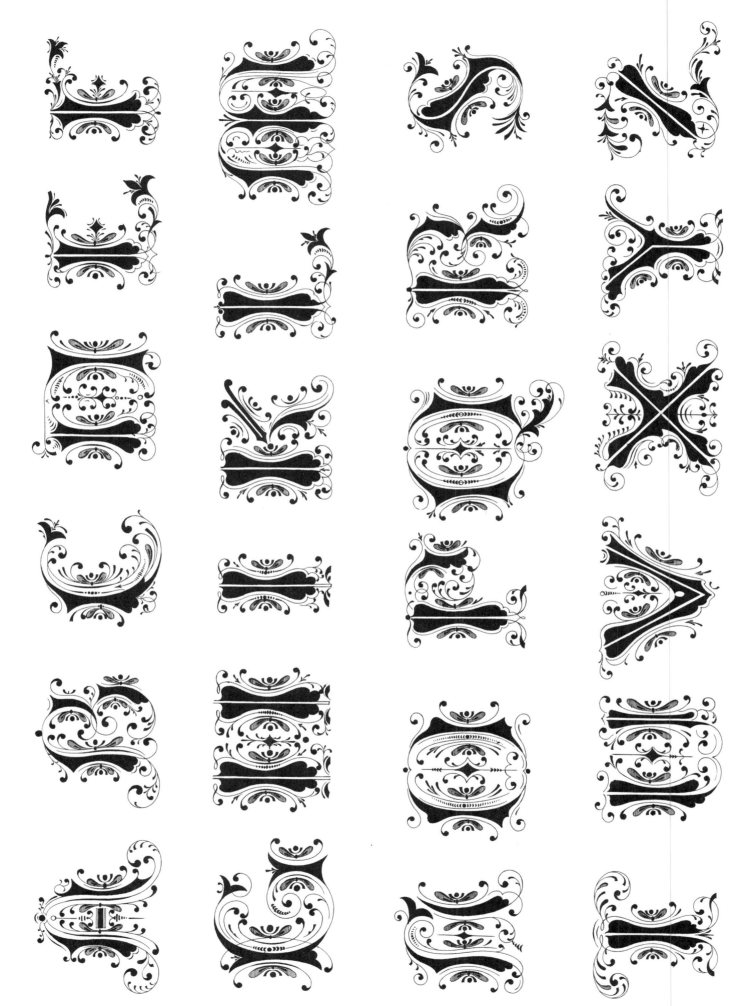

13   Midolle: "Gothic-Style Roman"

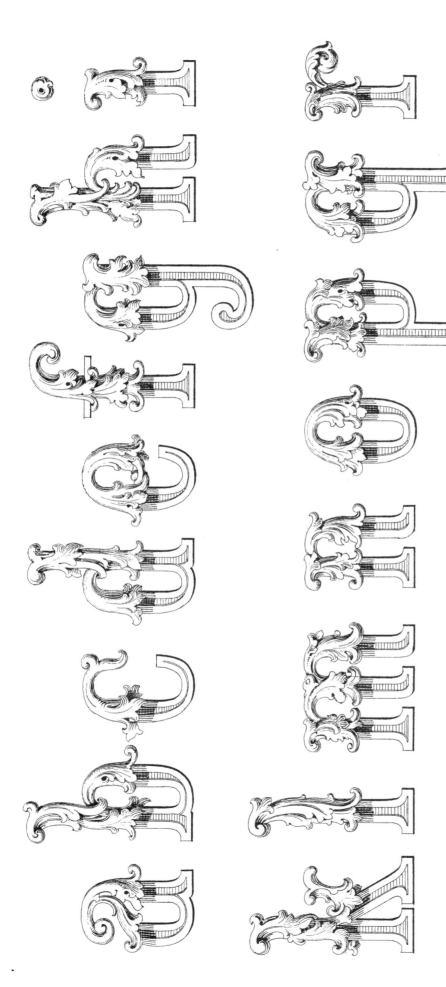

Klimsch

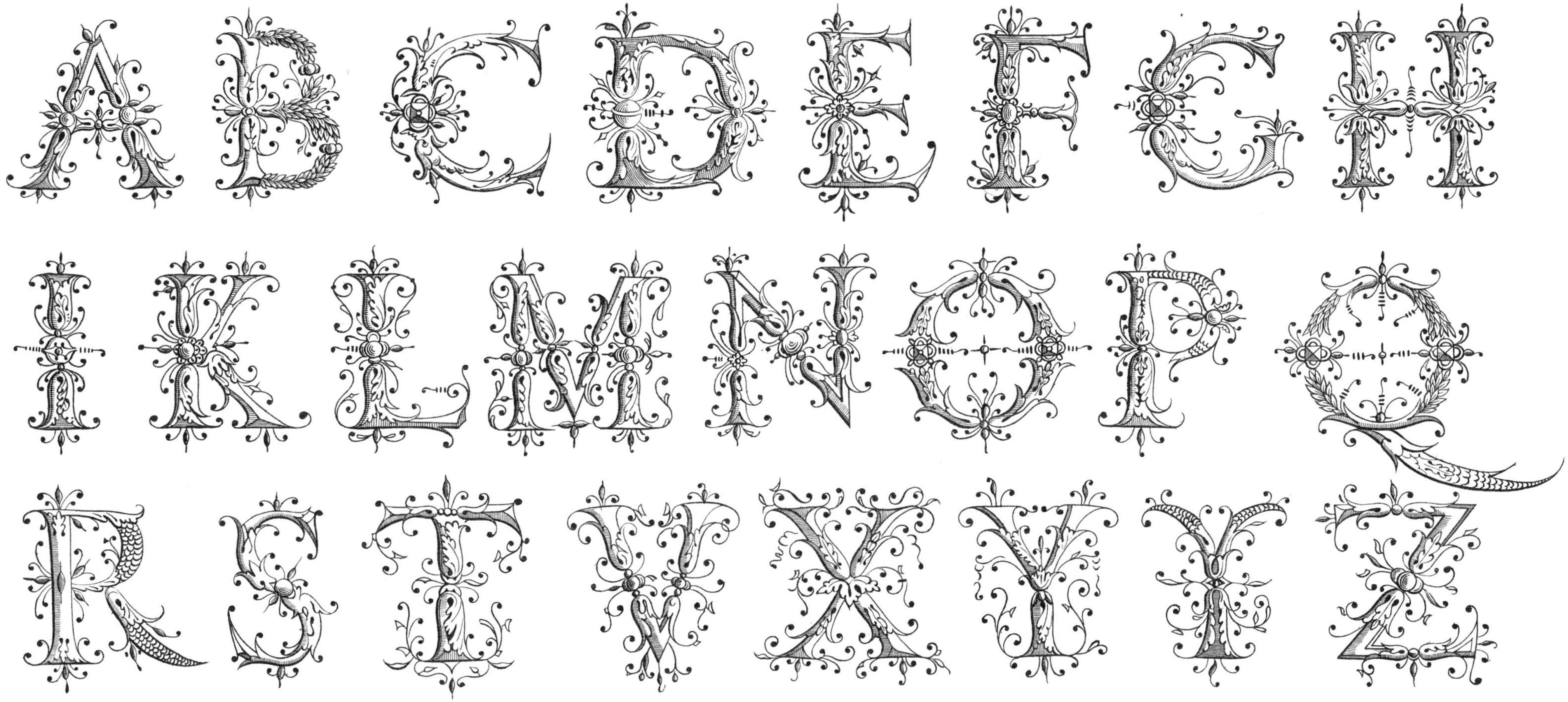

15 Silvestre: "16th Century; Italian; from a MS in the Library of St. Mark's, Venice"

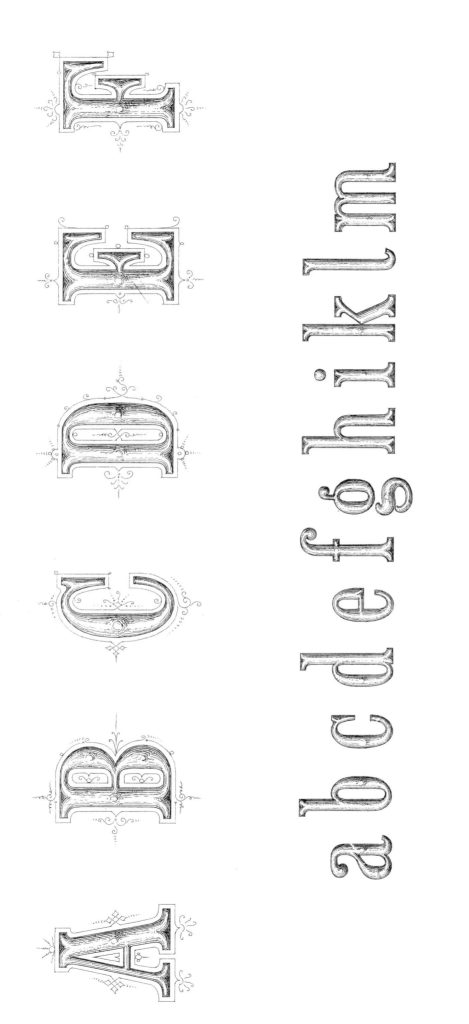

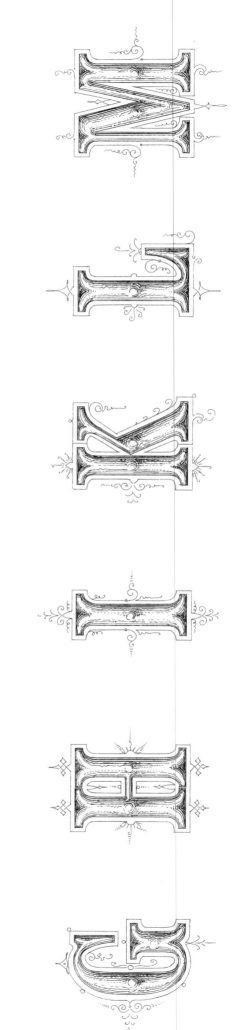

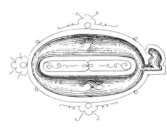

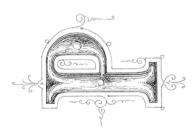

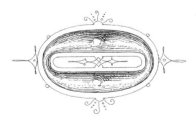

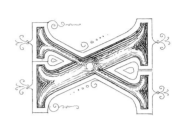

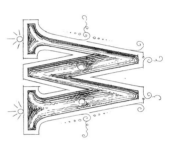

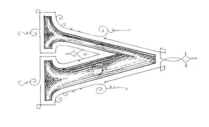

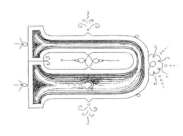

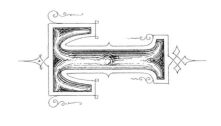

n o p q r s t u v w x z

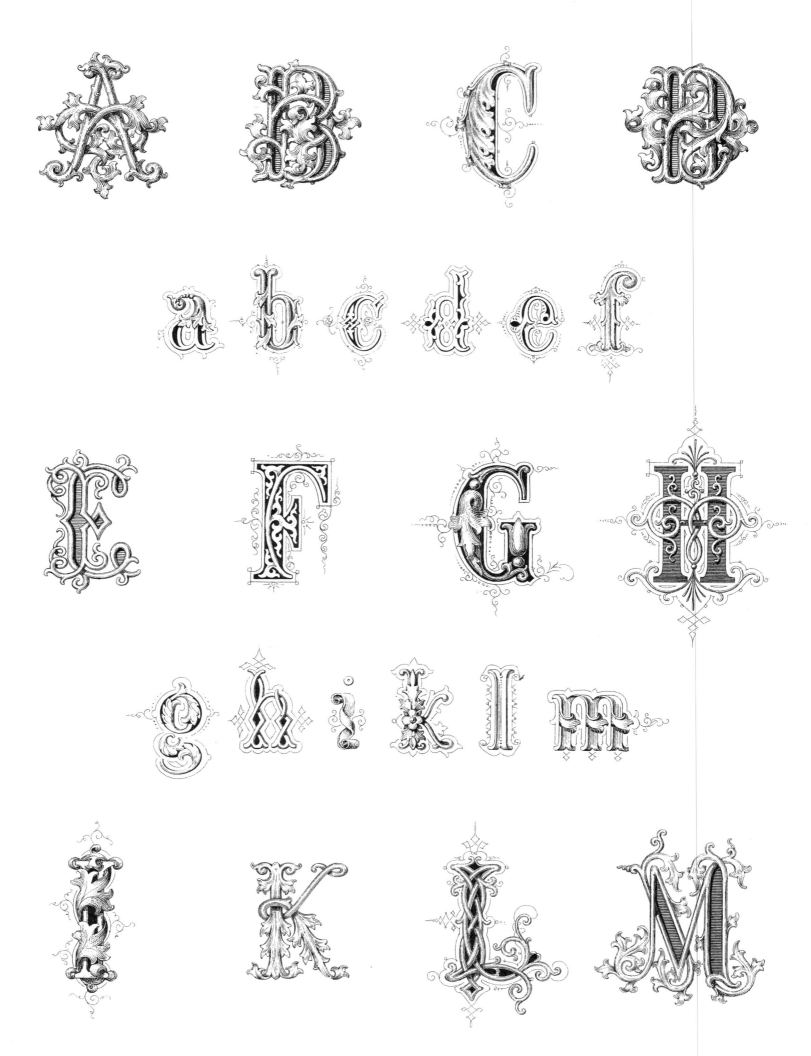

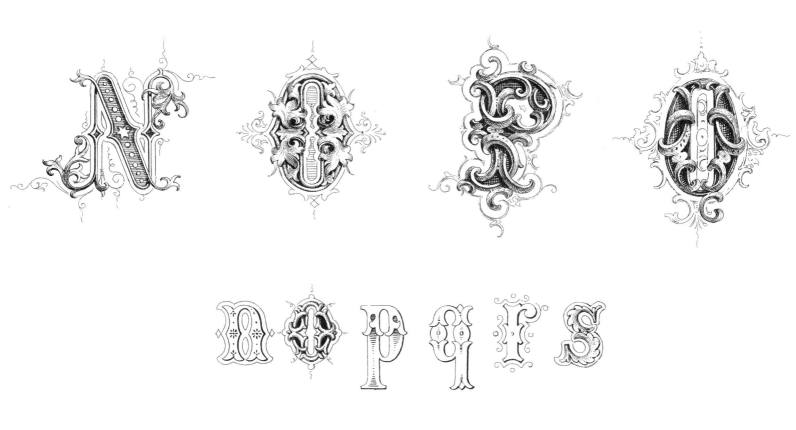

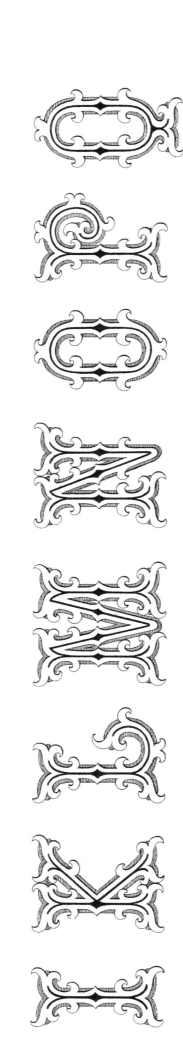

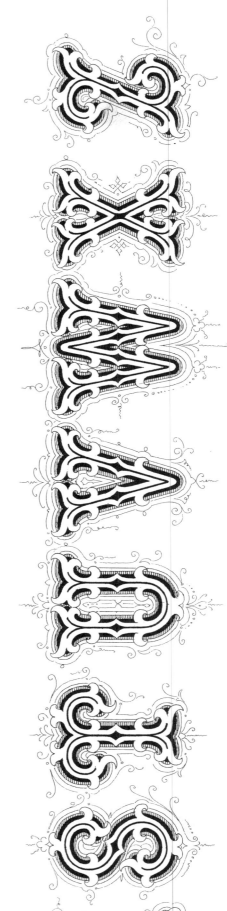

Klimsch

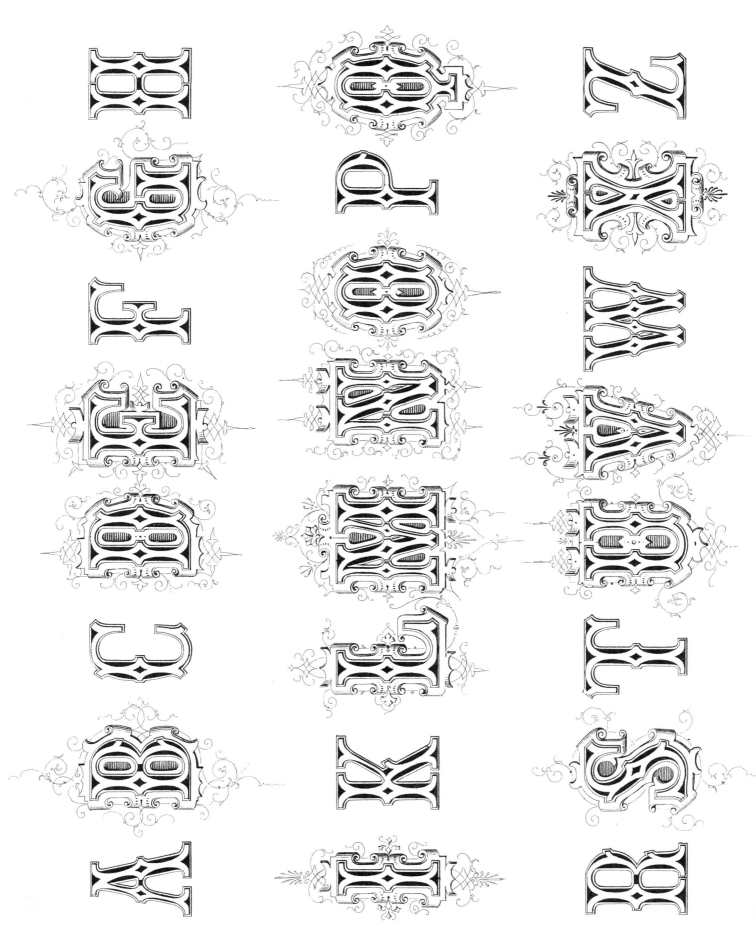

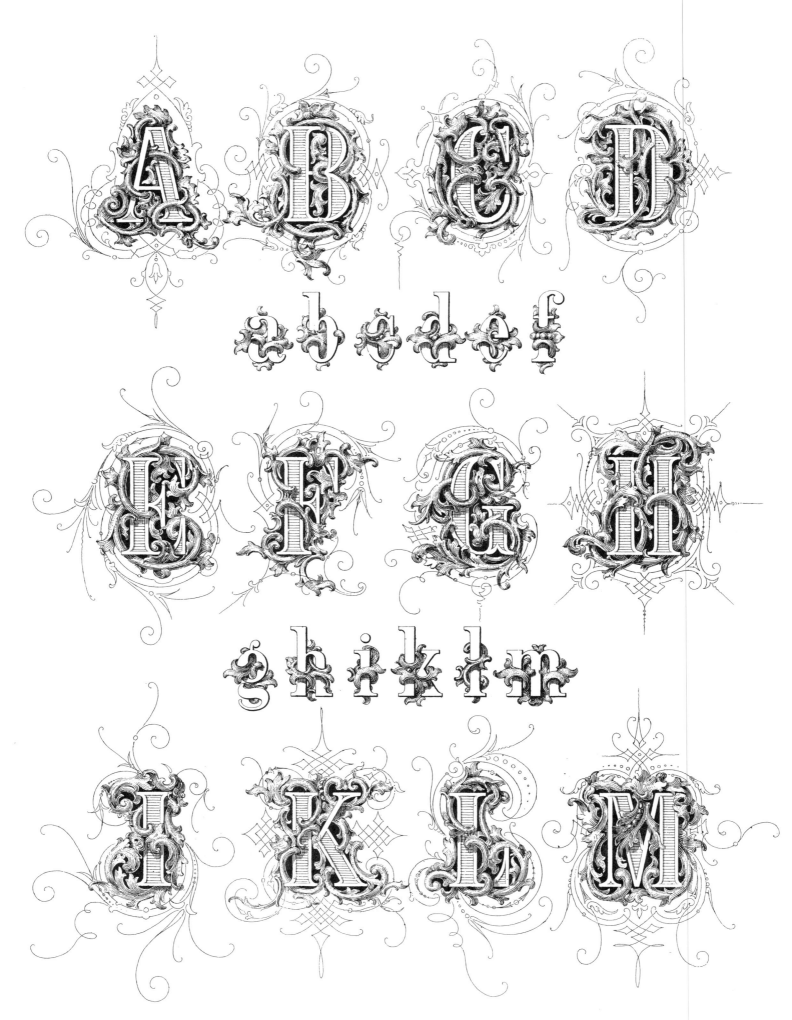

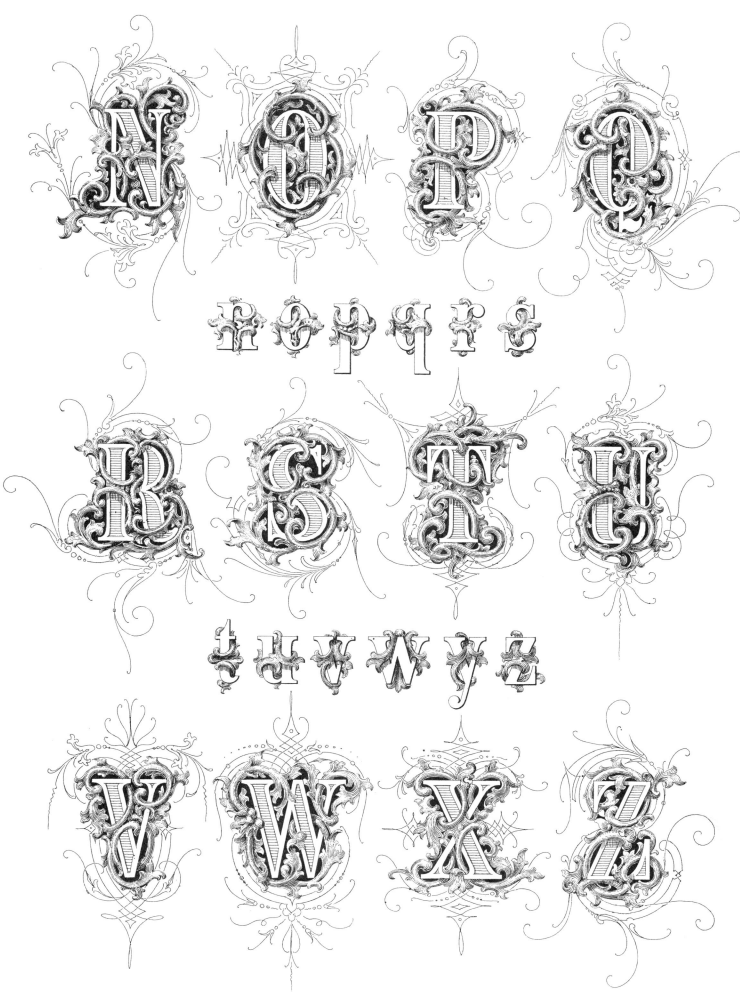

   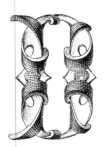

   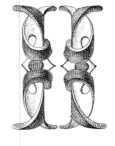

 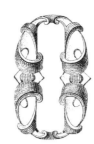  

   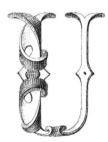

 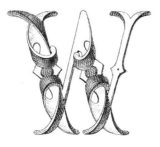  

Klimsch

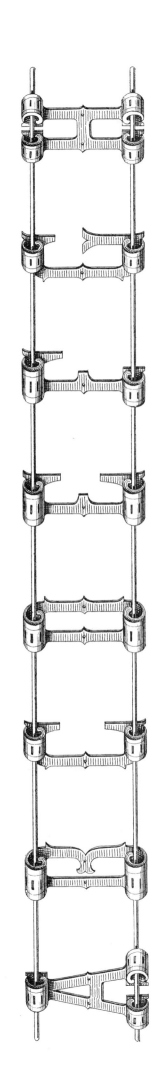
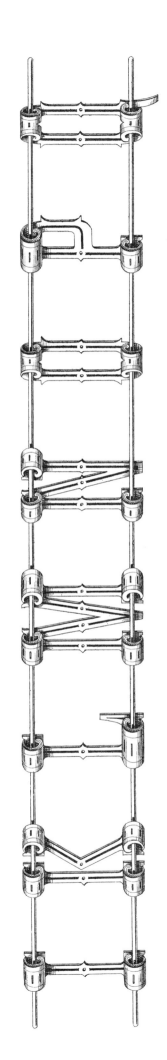
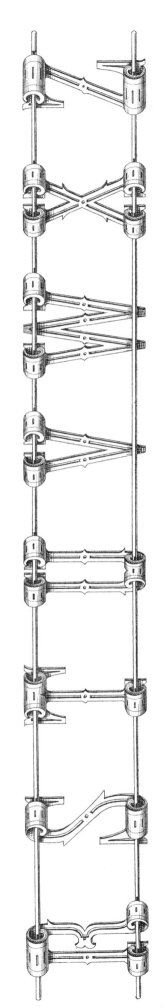

27   Klimsch

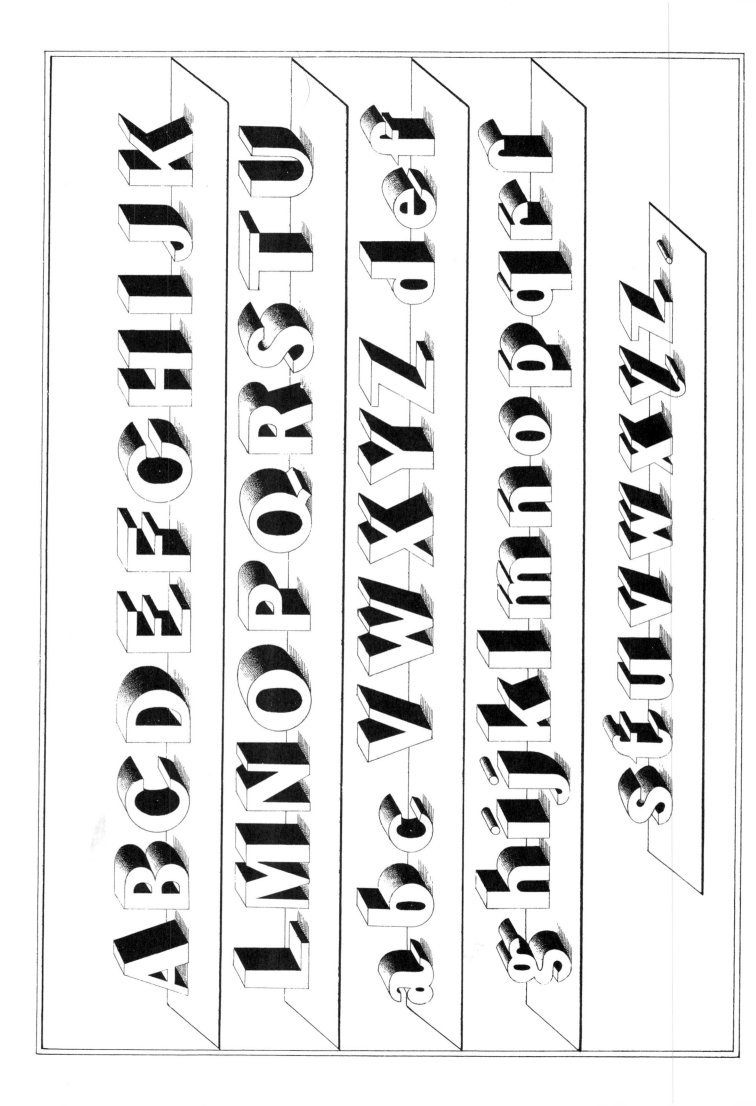

28   Silvestre: "19th Century; Wood-Carved Alphabet"

Midolle: "Monster Lapidary Alphabet"

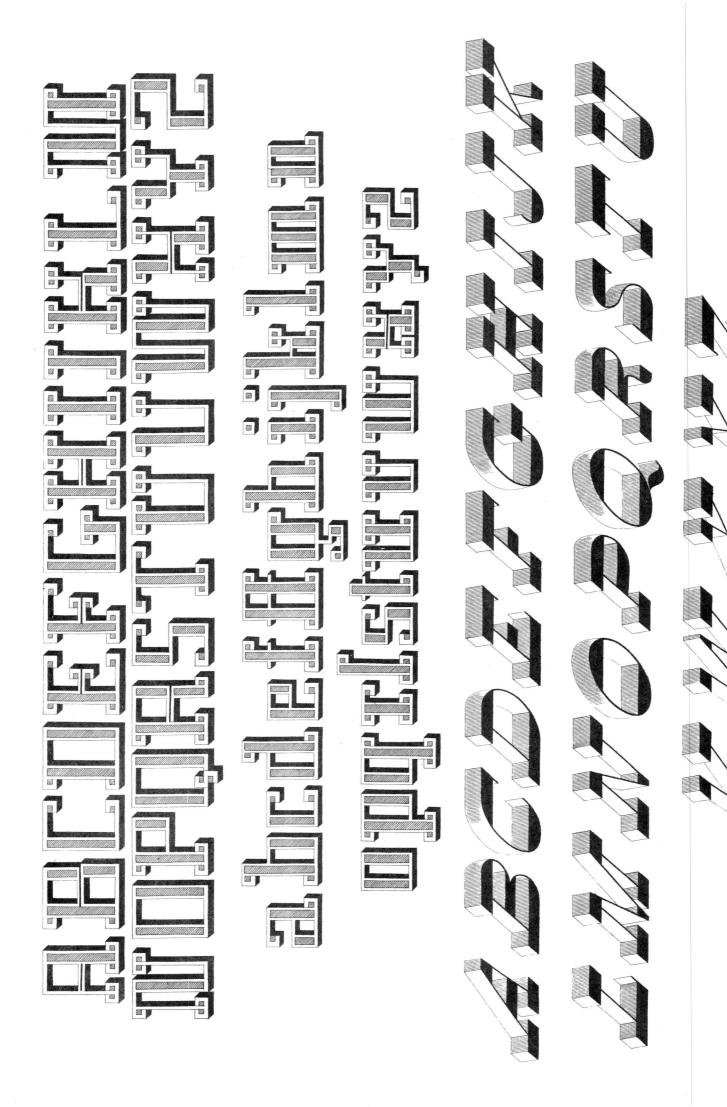

30   Silvestre: "19th Century; Imaginative Alphabets"

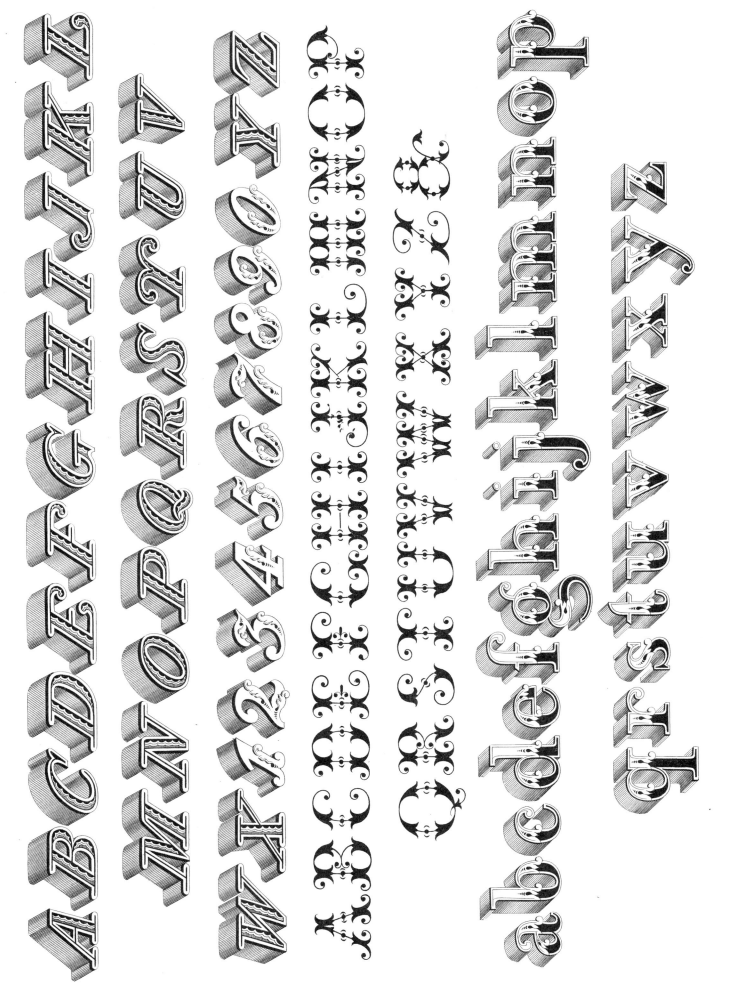

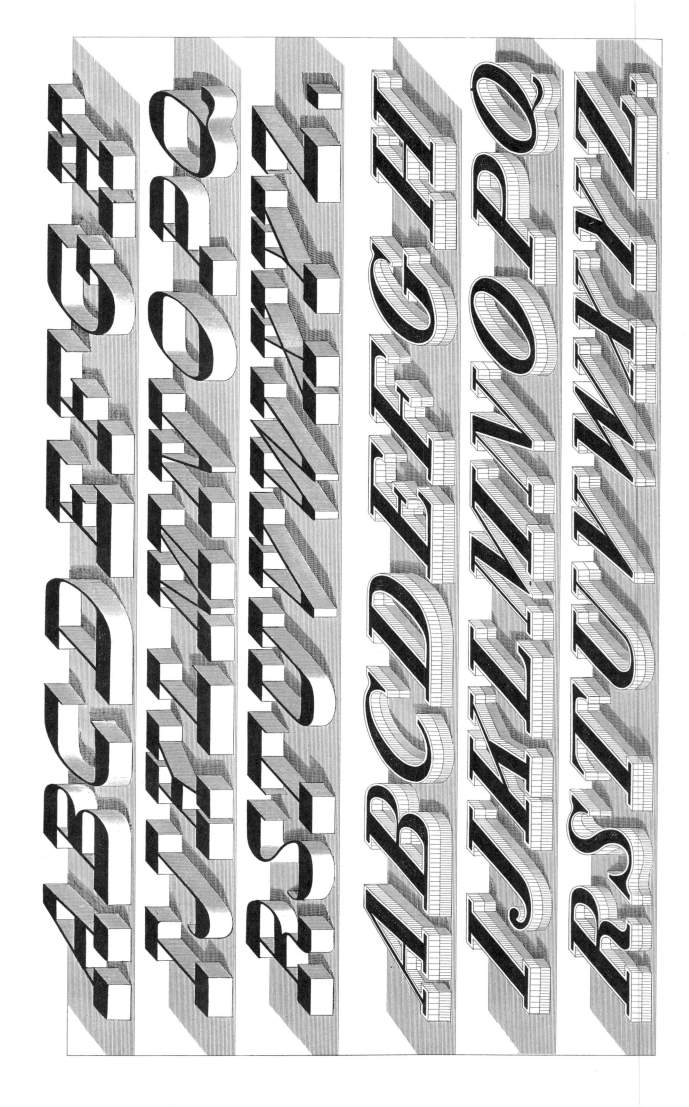

32   Silvestre: "19th Century; Reclining Capitals"

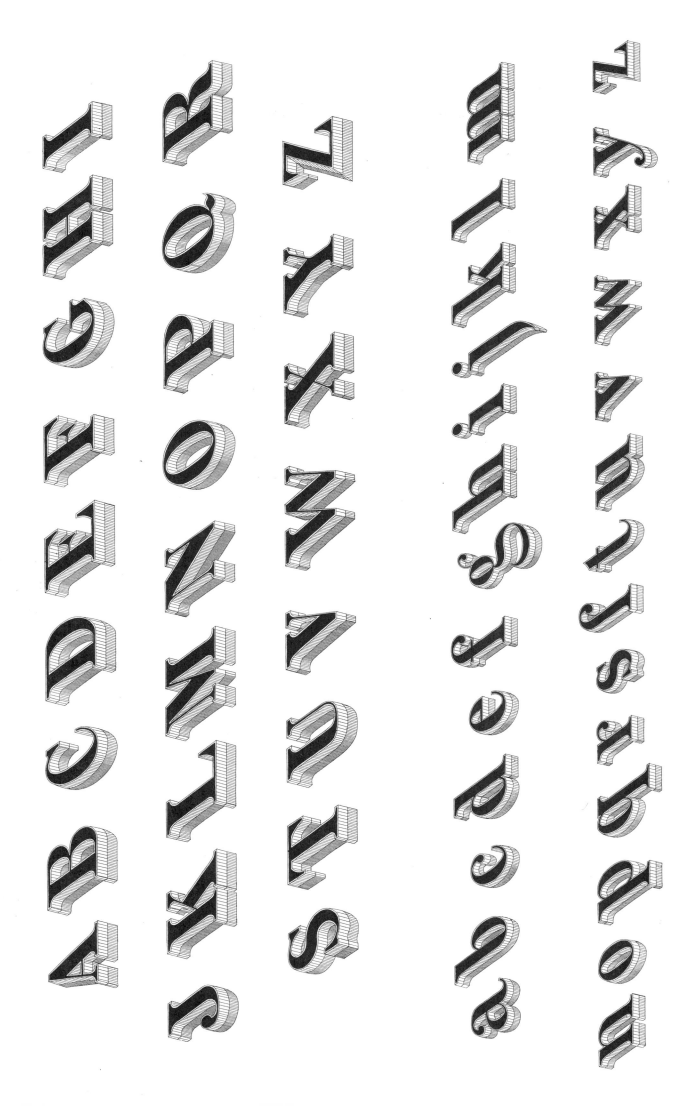

33 Silvestre: "19th Century; French; Inclined Three-Dimensional Letters"

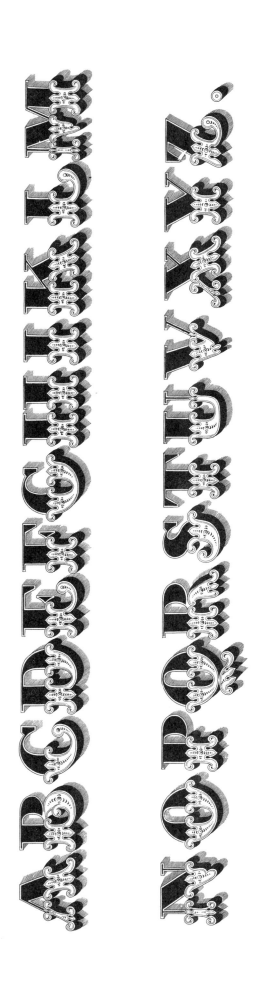

ABCDEFGHIJKLM
NOPQRSTUVWXYZ.

ABCDEFGHIJKLM
NOPQRSTUVWXYZ.

34   Silvestre: "19th Century; Imaginative Capitals"

35   Silvestre: "19th Century; Foliated Script Capitals"

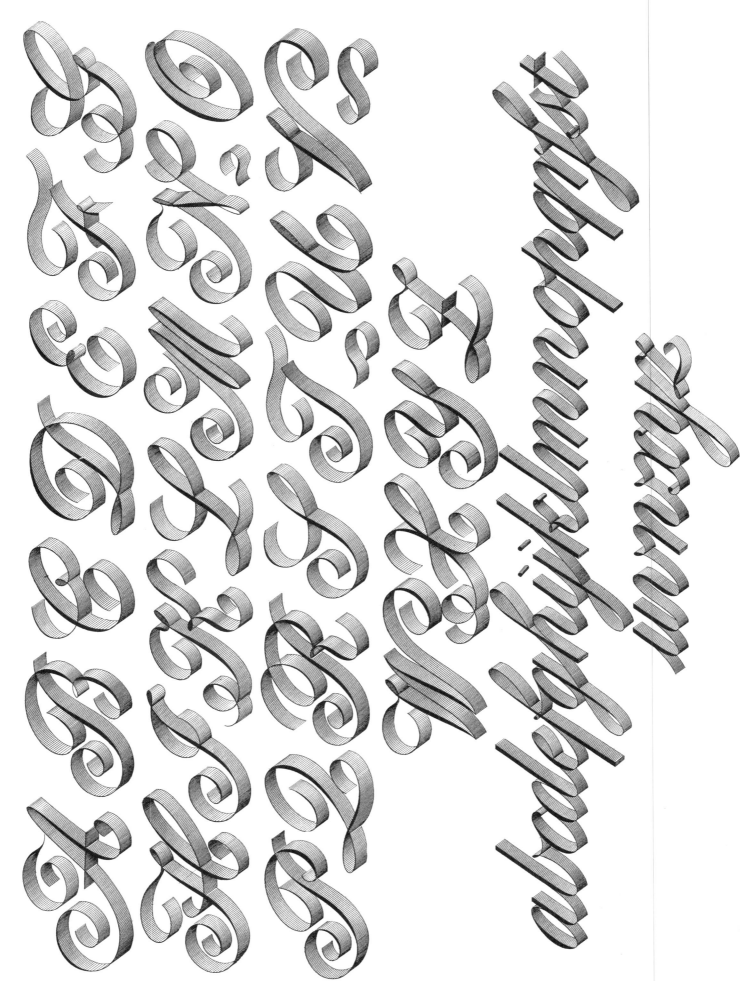

36   Silvestre: "19th Century; Ribbon Script Letters"

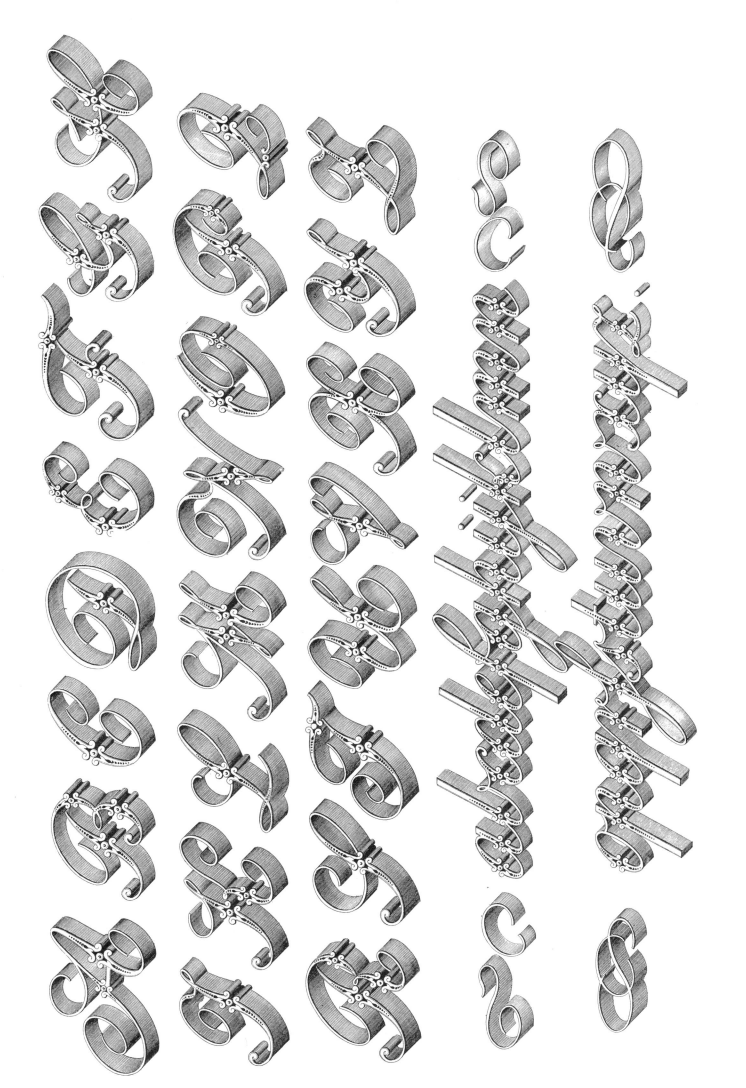

37 Silvestre: "19th Century; Ribbon Script Letters"

ALPHABET

de l'Écriture Française

à la fin du 16.ᵐᵉ Siècle.

abcdefghijklmno

pqrſſstuvwxyz & bd

D'après Guillaume Legangneur

Sécrétaire ordinaire de la Chambre du Roi.

1599

ESCRITURA REDONDA

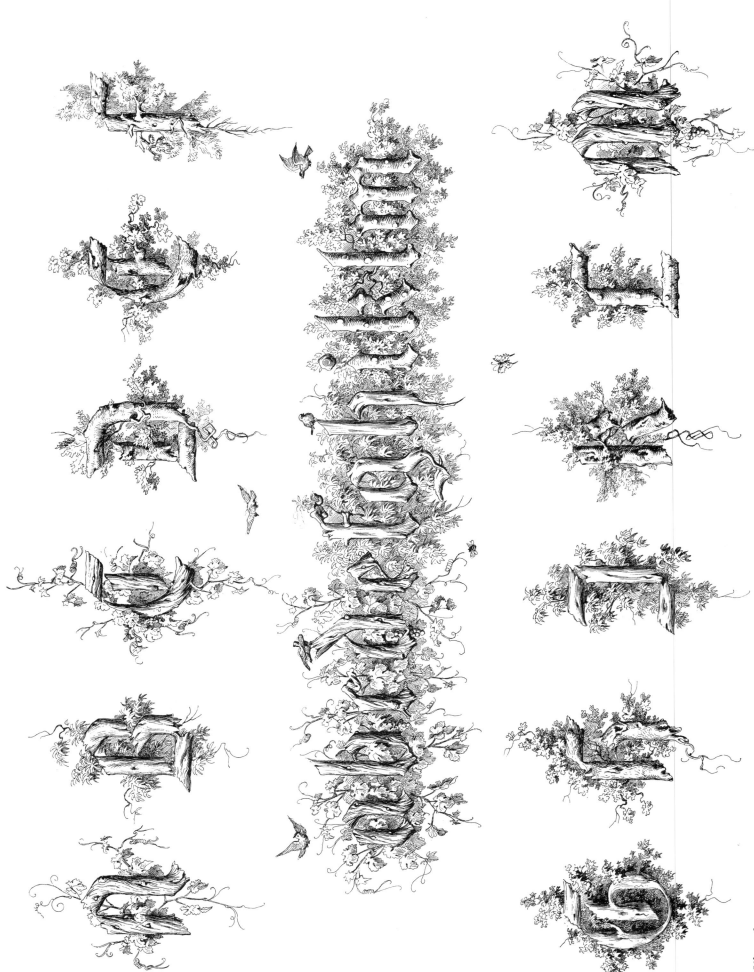

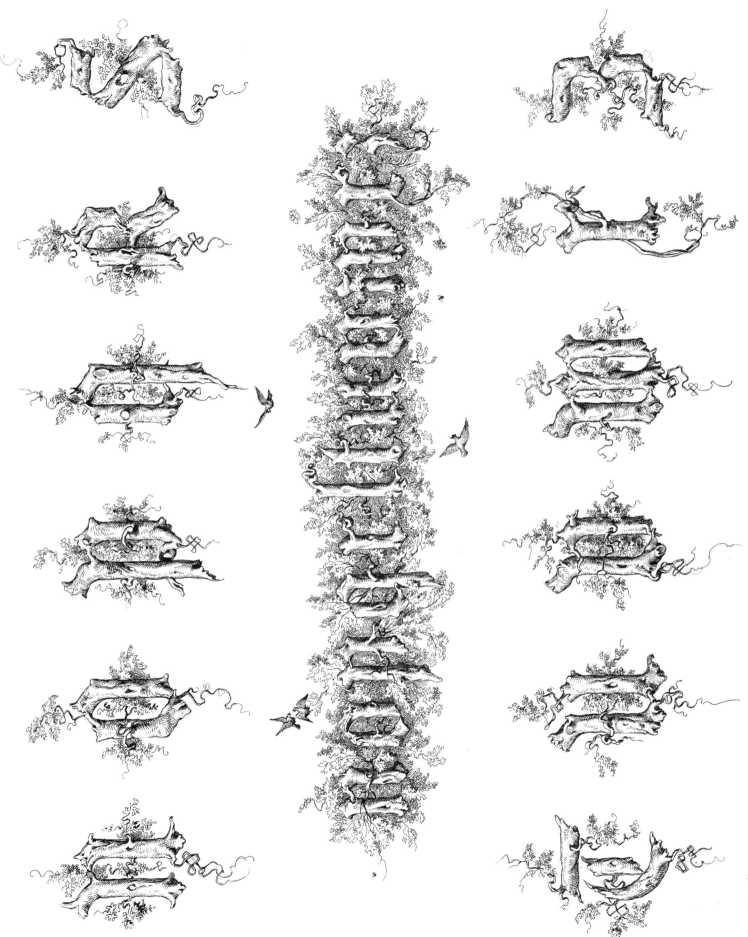

44   Silvestre: "19th Century; French; Animal Alphabet"

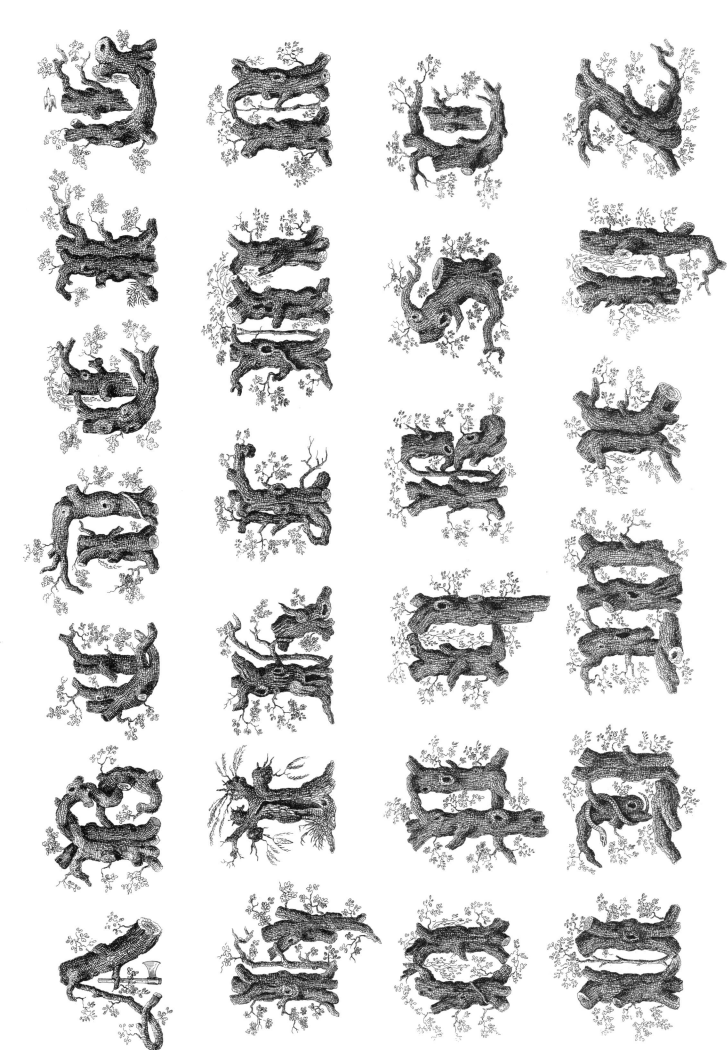

45   Silvestre: "19th Century; French; Tree Alphabet"

46   Silvestre: "17th Century: Italian; Human-Figure Alphabet; Paris Royal Library (Fontanieu)"

ALPHABET DIABOLIQUE.

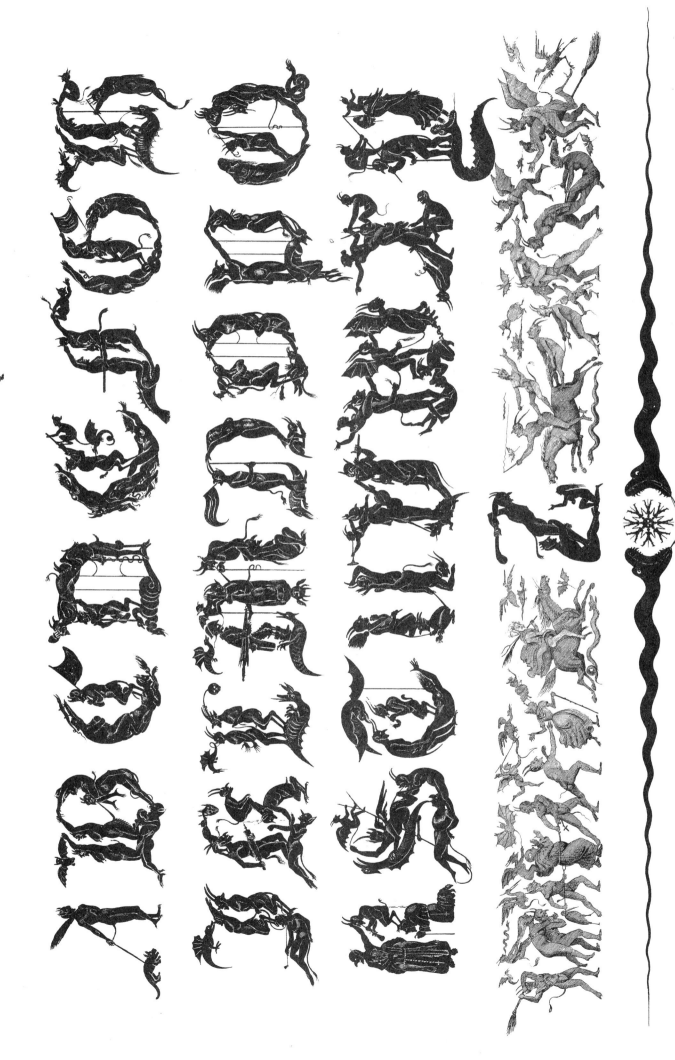

Midolle

48   Midolle: "Imaginative Alphabet Based on Greek Ornament"

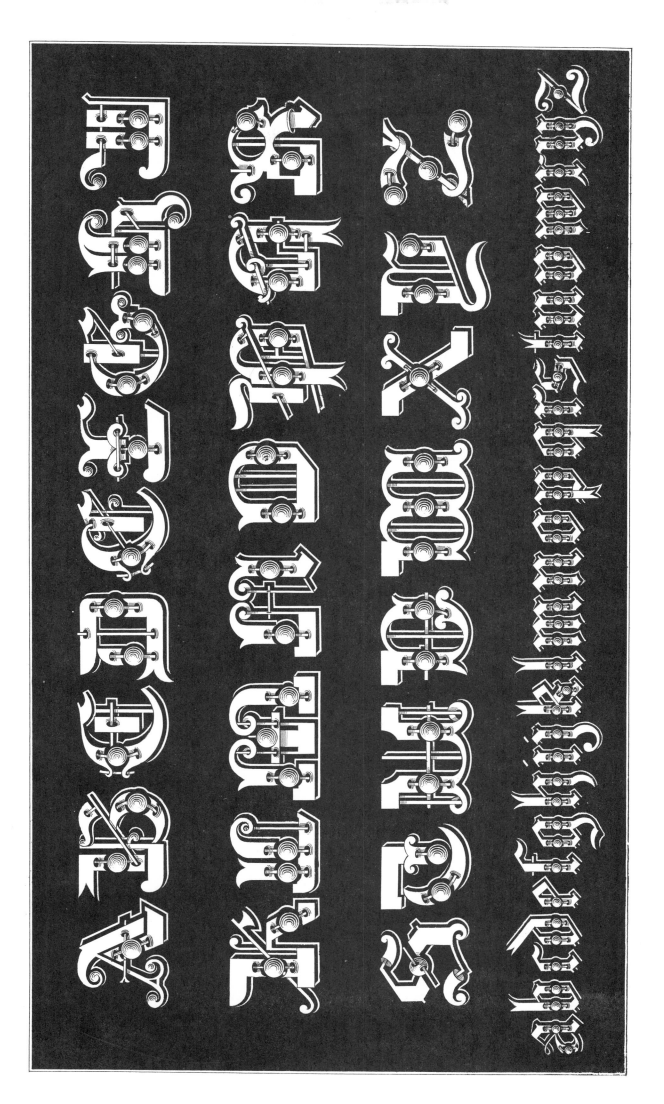

49   Silvestre: "15th Century; Italian; Lapidary Alphabet from Turin"

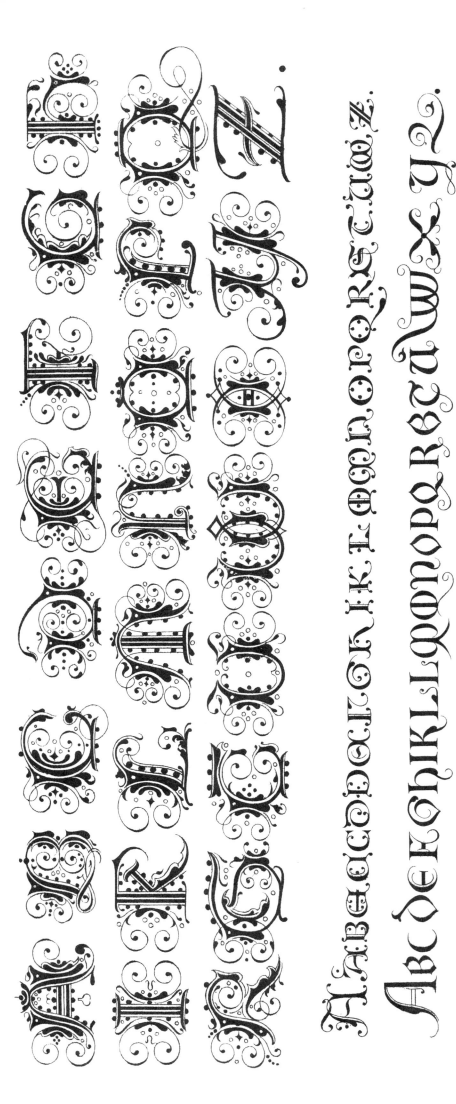

50 Silvestre: "12th Century; German; MS in the Munich Royal Library"

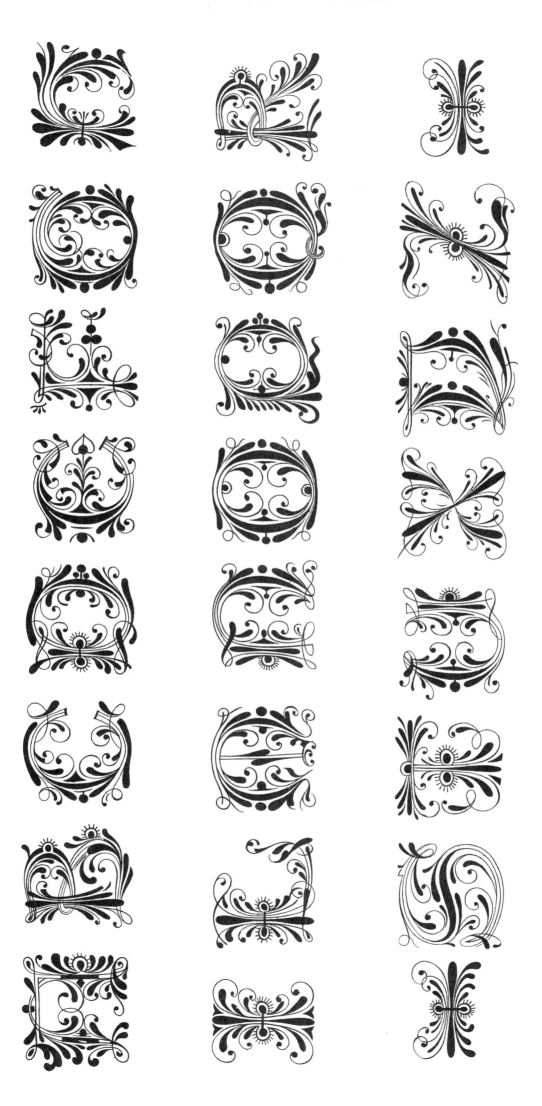

51   Silvestre: "15th Century; Italian; from a Venetian MS"

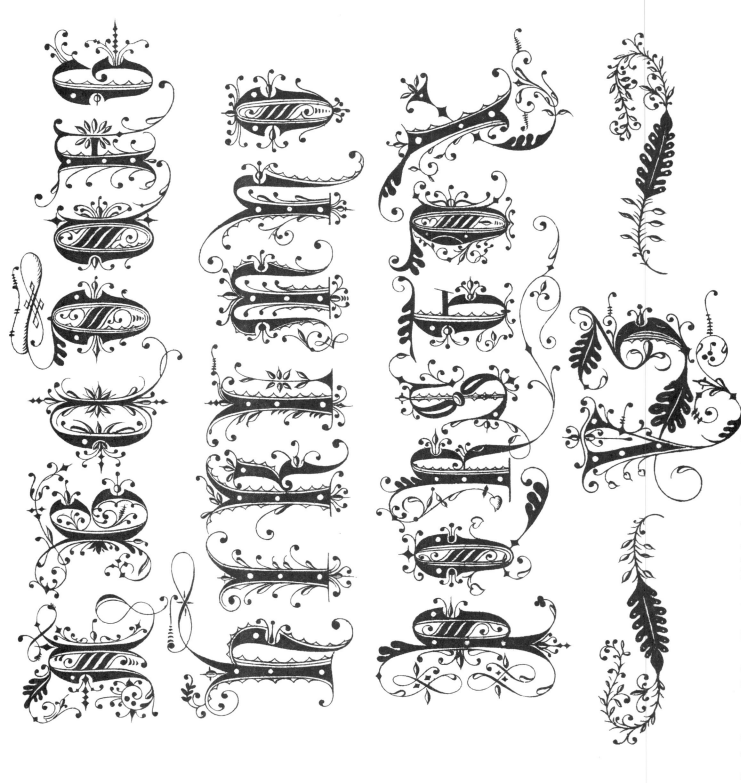

Silvestre: "17th Century; Italian; Venetian Alphabet by Vespasiano"

Silvestre: "18th Century; German; from a MS in Vienna"

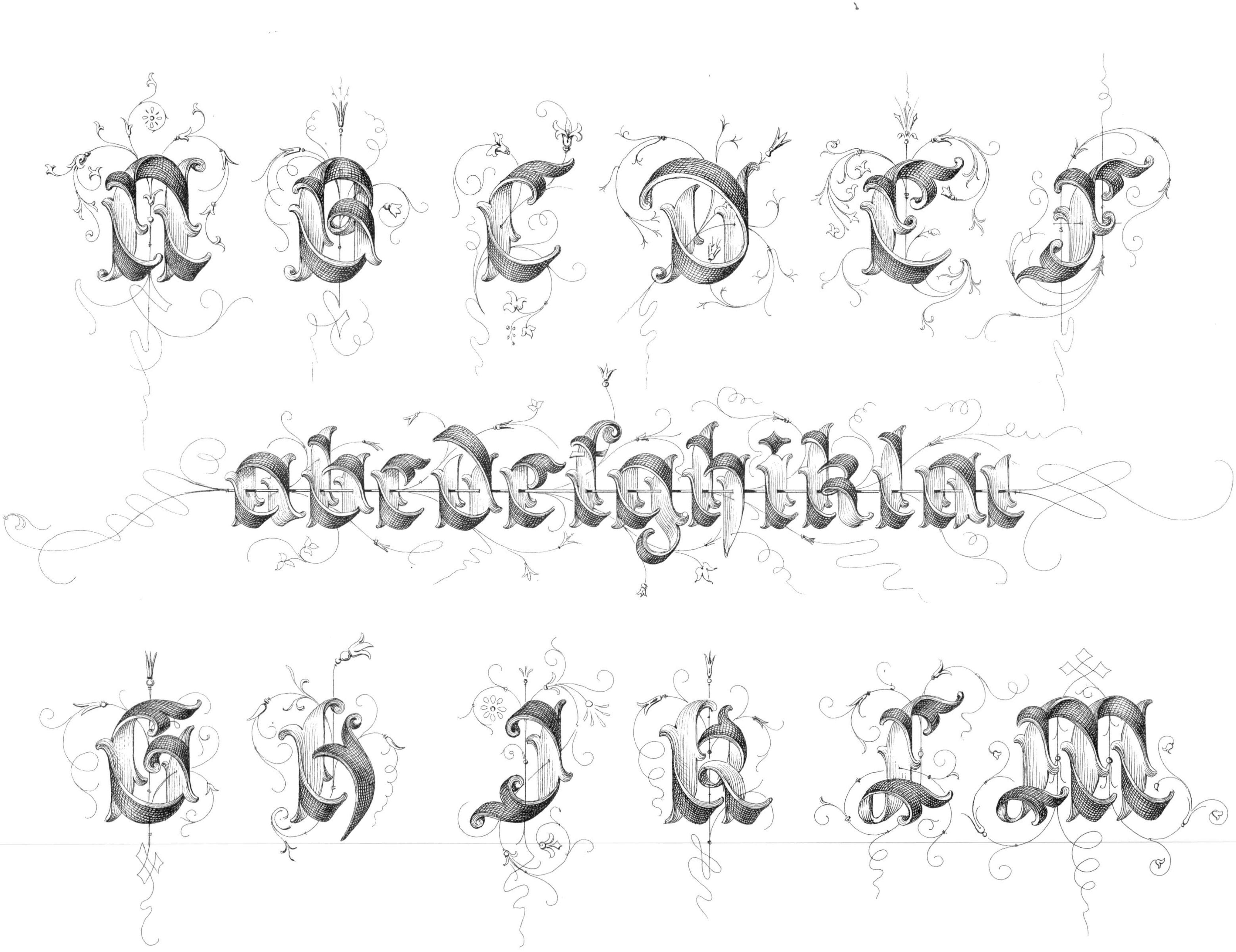

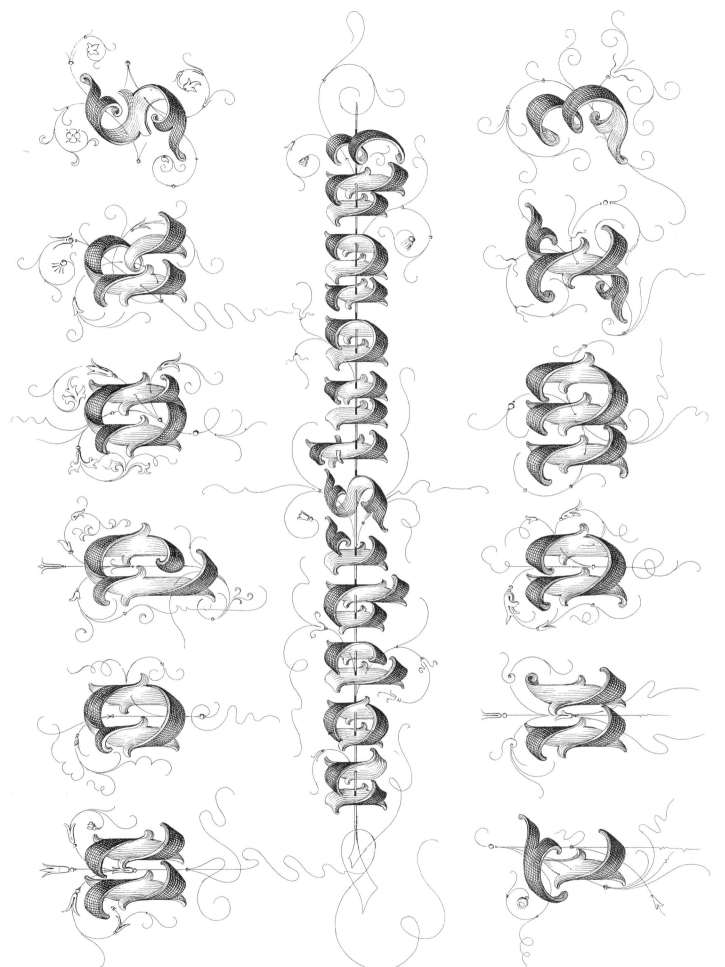

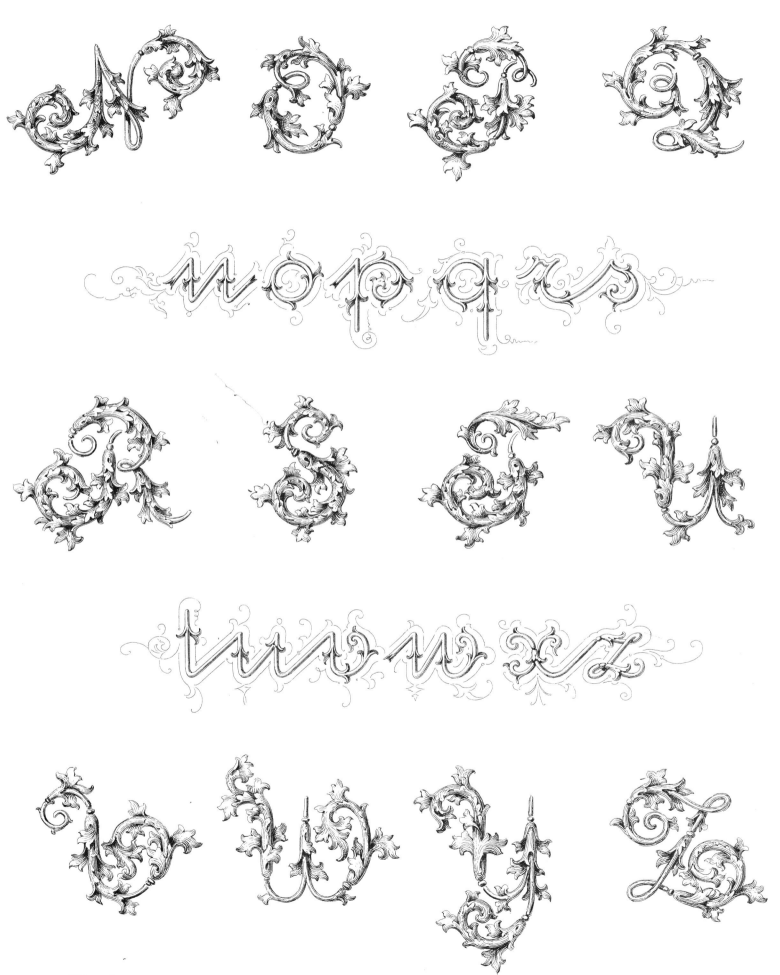

58   Silvestre: "18th Century; Italian; Alphabet by Tagliente"

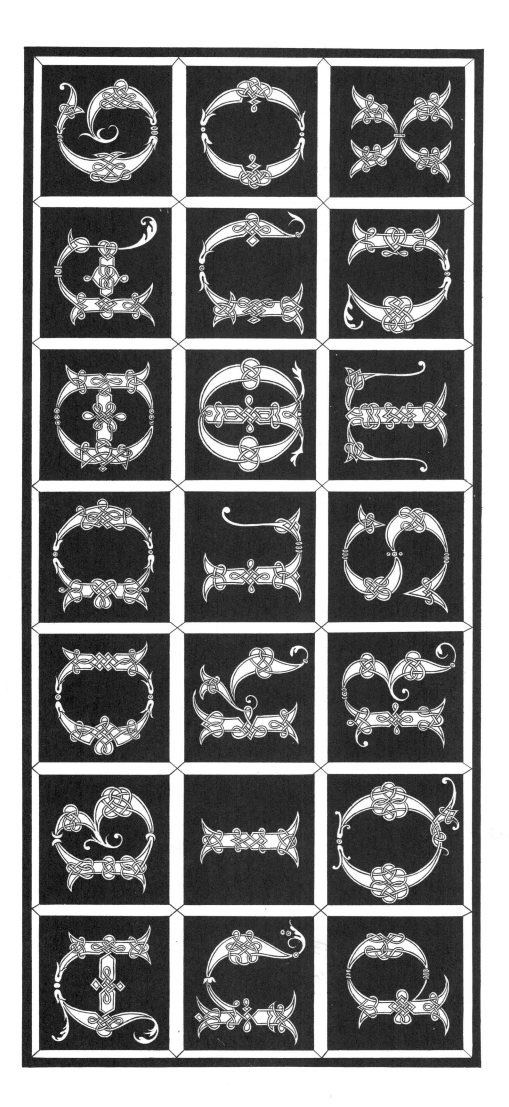

59   Silvestre: "16th Century; Italian; Alphabet by Tagliente in the Vatican Library"

A B C D E F G H I J K L M N O P Q R S T U V W X Y Z

abcdefghijklmnopqrstuvwxyz

60   Midolle: "Italian Ecclesiastical Script"

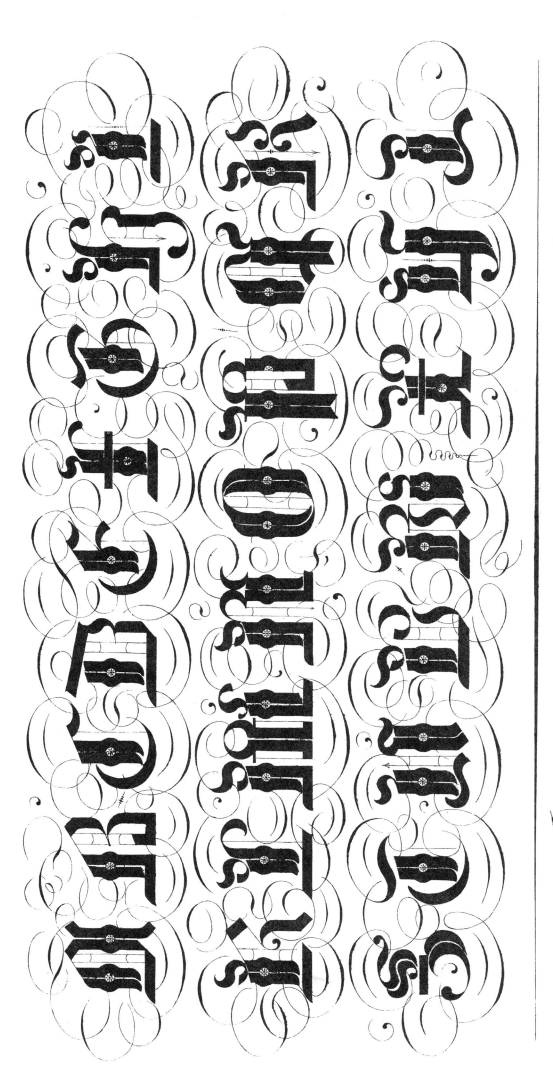

61   Midolle: "Gothic; from the Pisan Charters, 1500"

Silvestre: "14th Century; Italian; from a Missal in the Vatican Library"

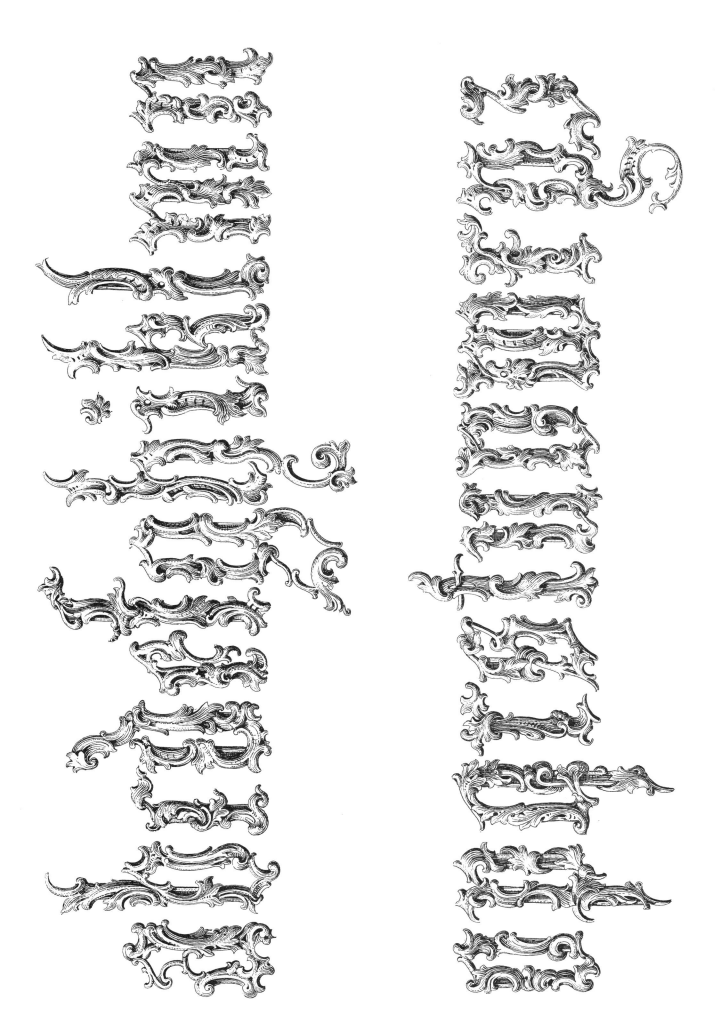

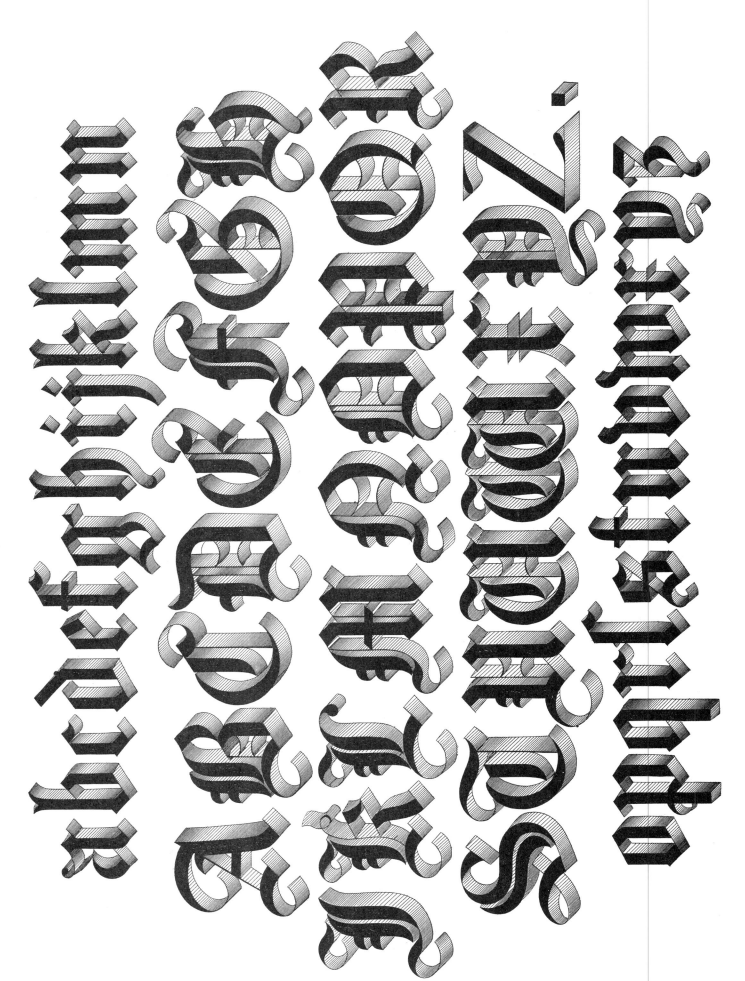

64   Silvestre: "19th Century; German; Three-Dimensional Gothic Alphabet"

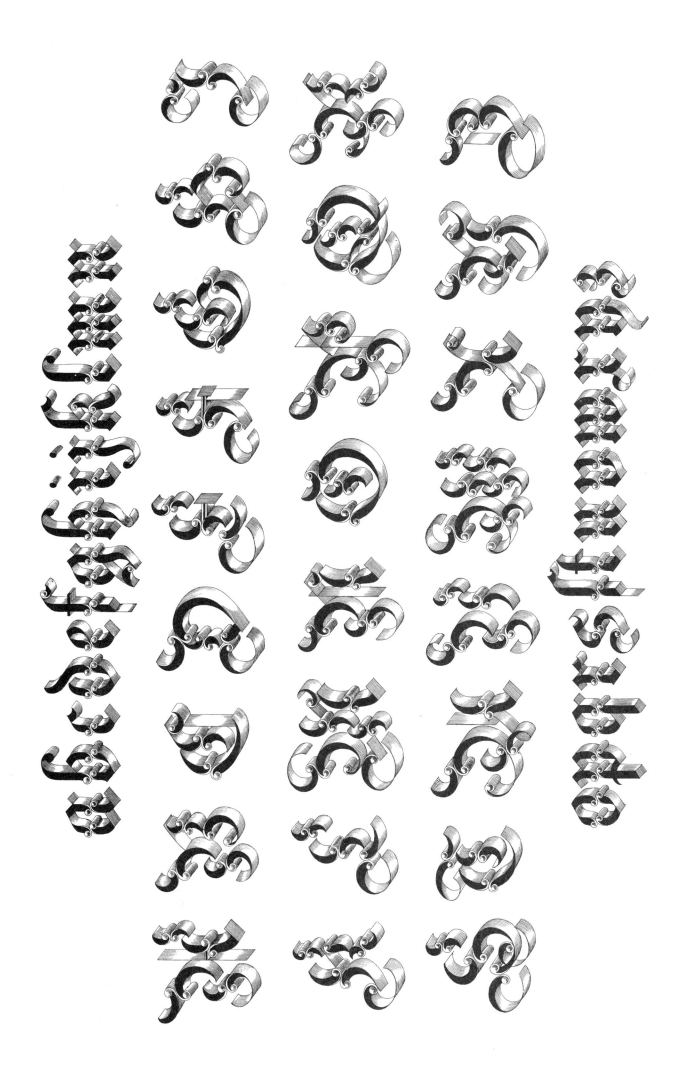

Silvestre: "19th Century; English; Segmented Gothic Letters"

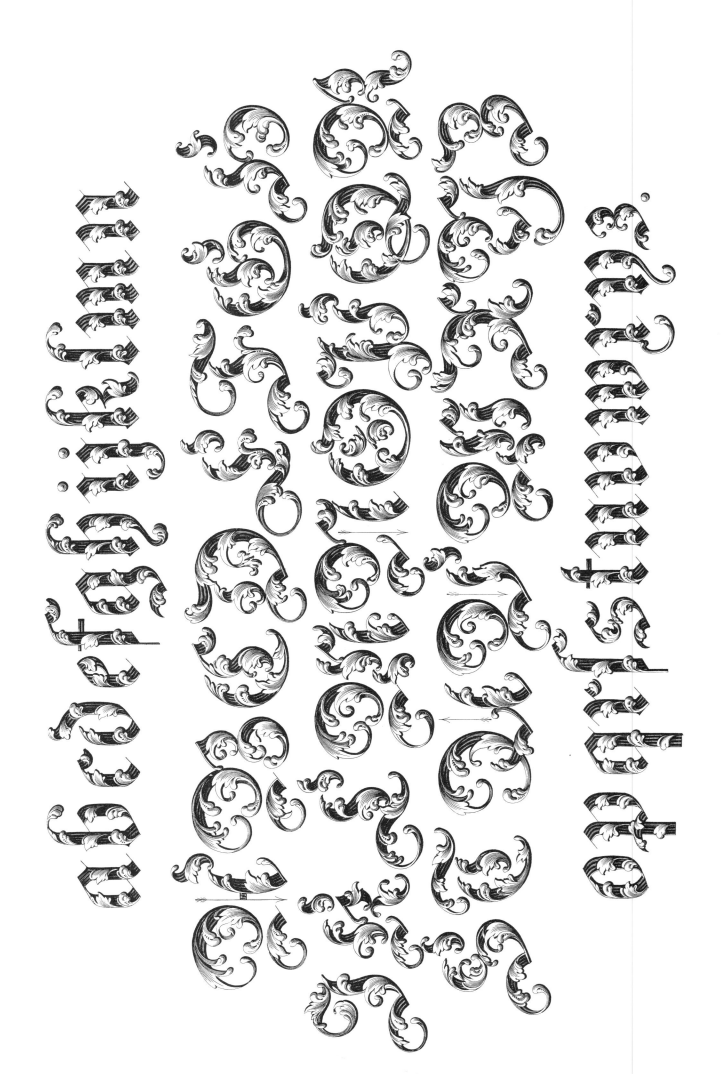

66   Silvestre: "19th Century; Foliated Gothic Alphabet"

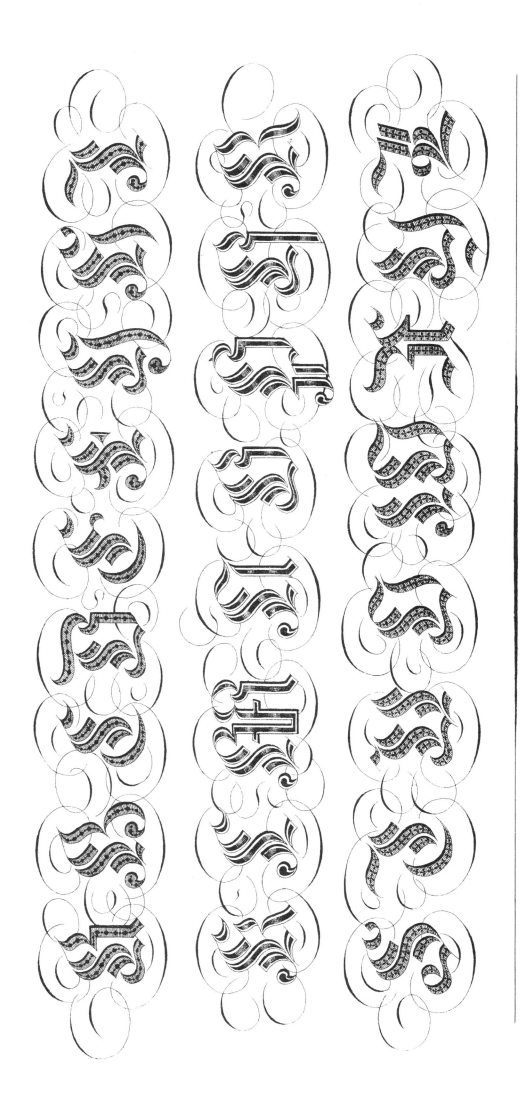

abcdefghijklmnopqrstuvwxyz

68   Midolle: "Margrave Gothic"

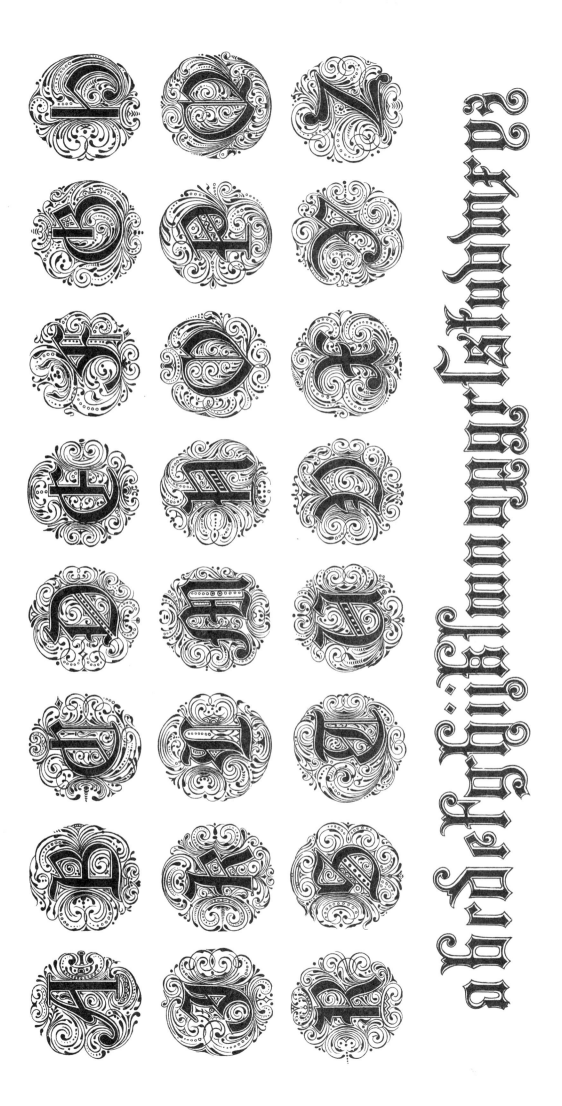

69 Silvestre: "14th Century; German; from a MS in Vienna"

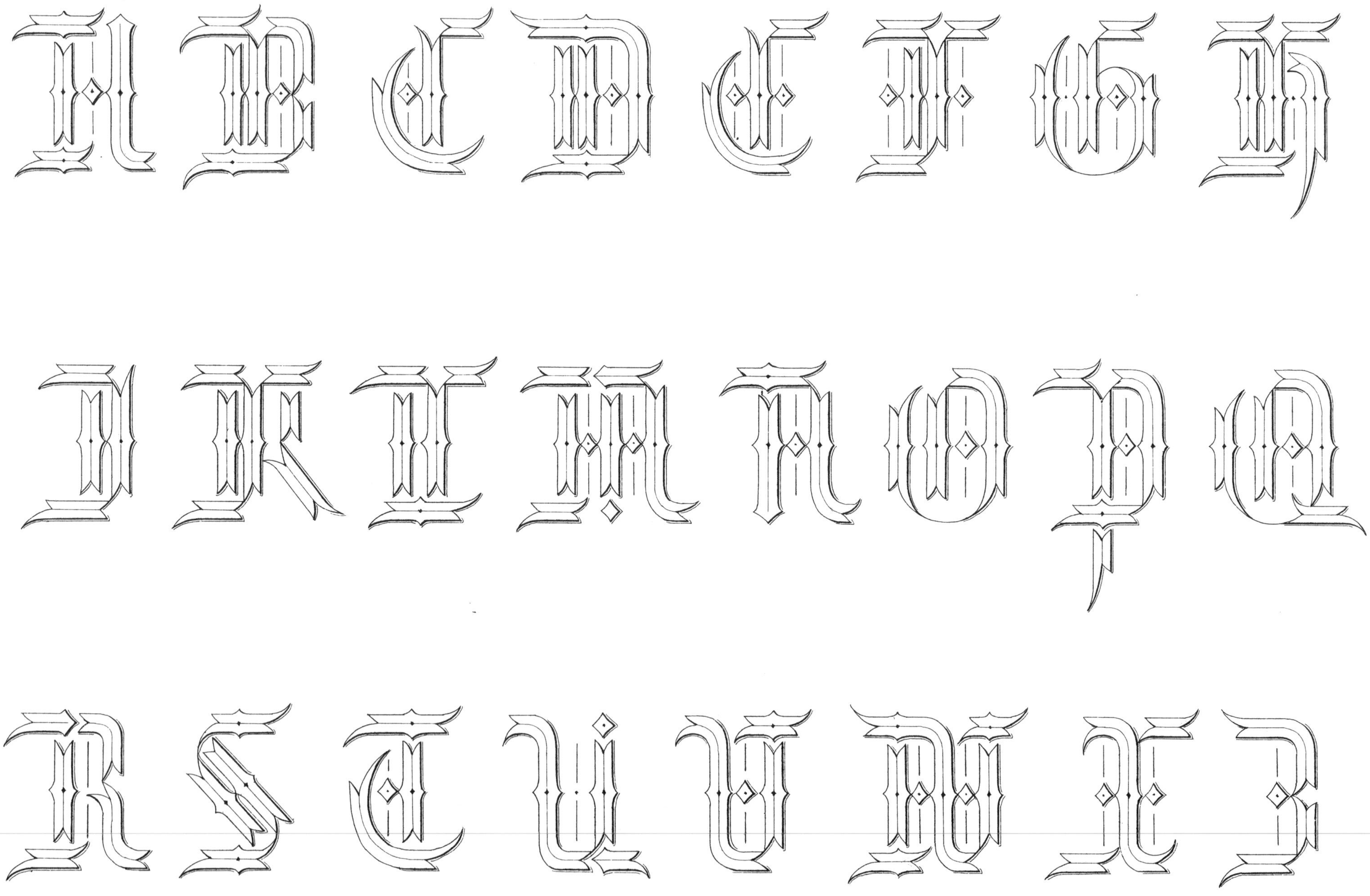

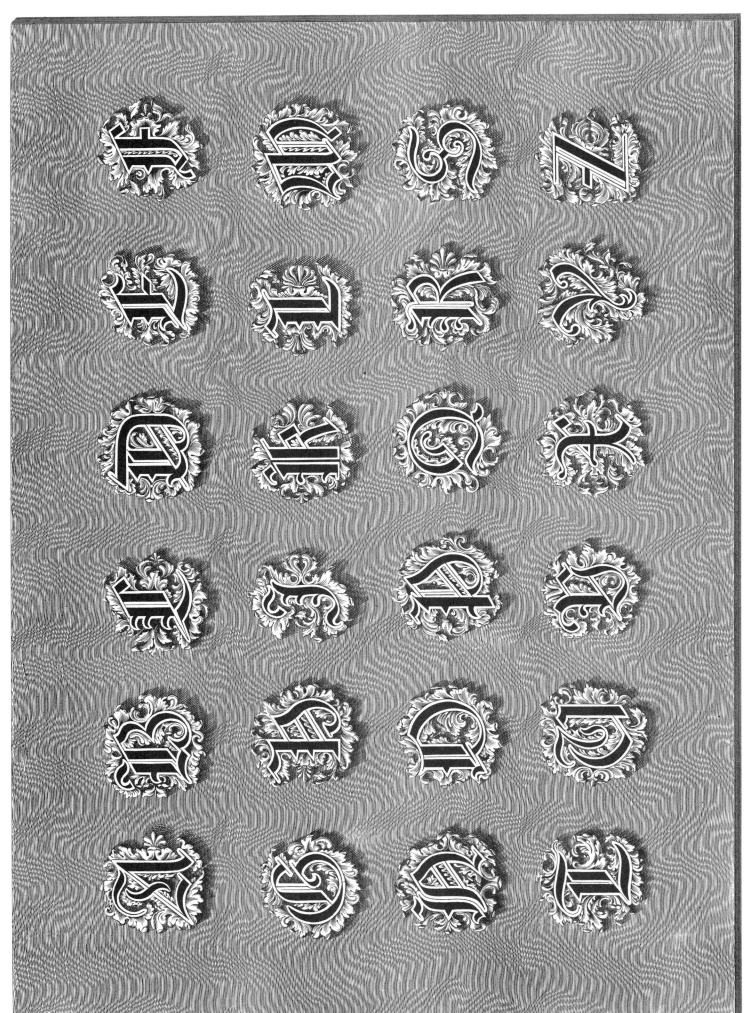

71   Silvestre: "14th Century; German; from a MS in the Munich Royal Library"

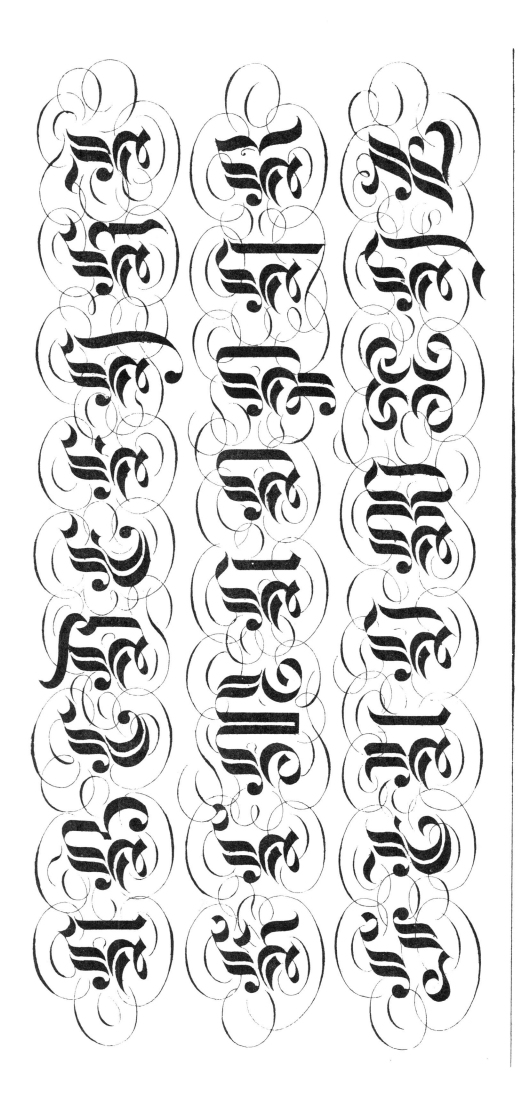

abcdefghiklmnopqrstuwxyz

Midolle: "Midolle's Fraktur"

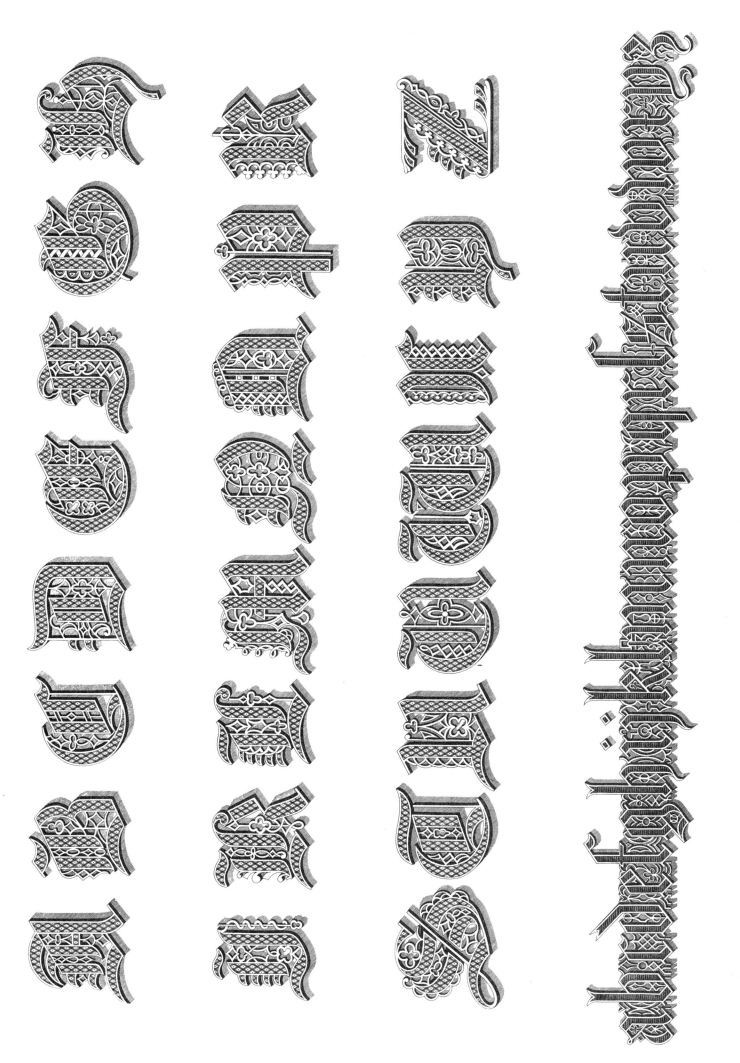

73   Silvestre: "15th Century; German; Decorative Gothic Letters; from the Venice Library"

74   Silvestre: "17th Century; Italian; Alphabet by Vespasiano; Library of St. Mark's, Venice"

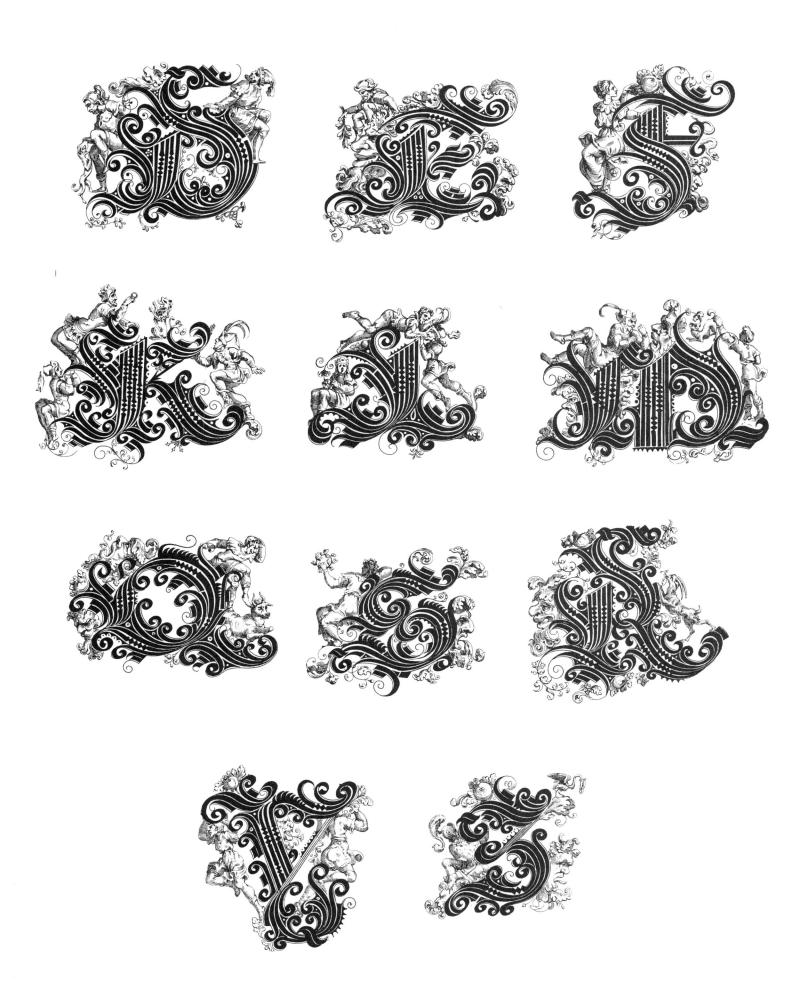

GOTHIQUE COMPOSÉE.

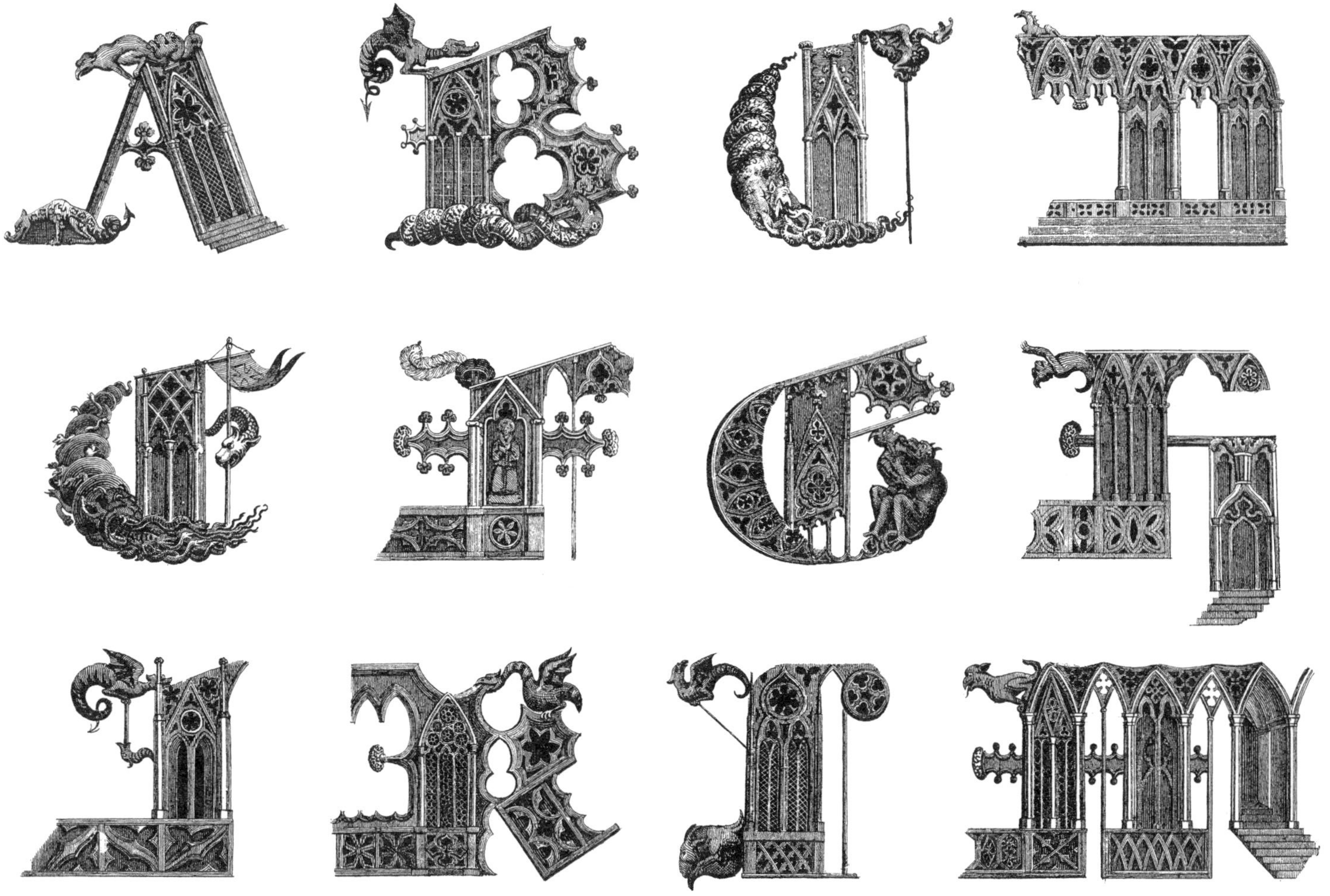

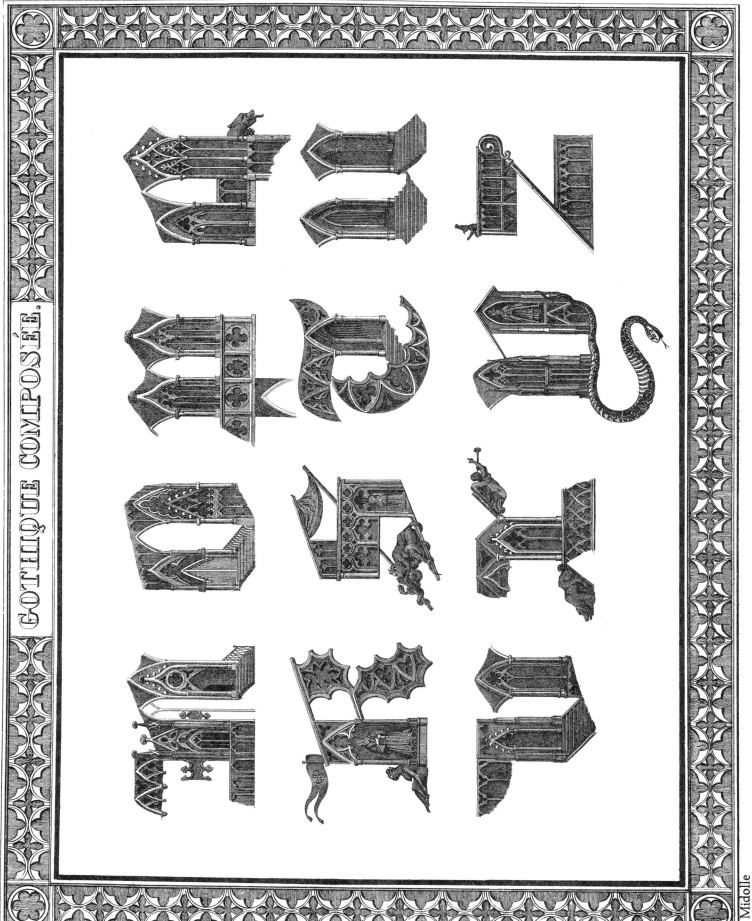

Midolle

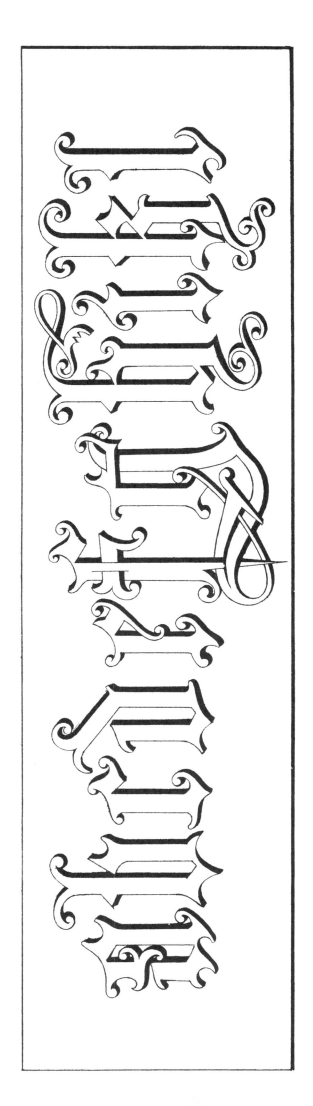

78   Silvestre: "16th Century; German; Gothic Lapidary Alphabet"

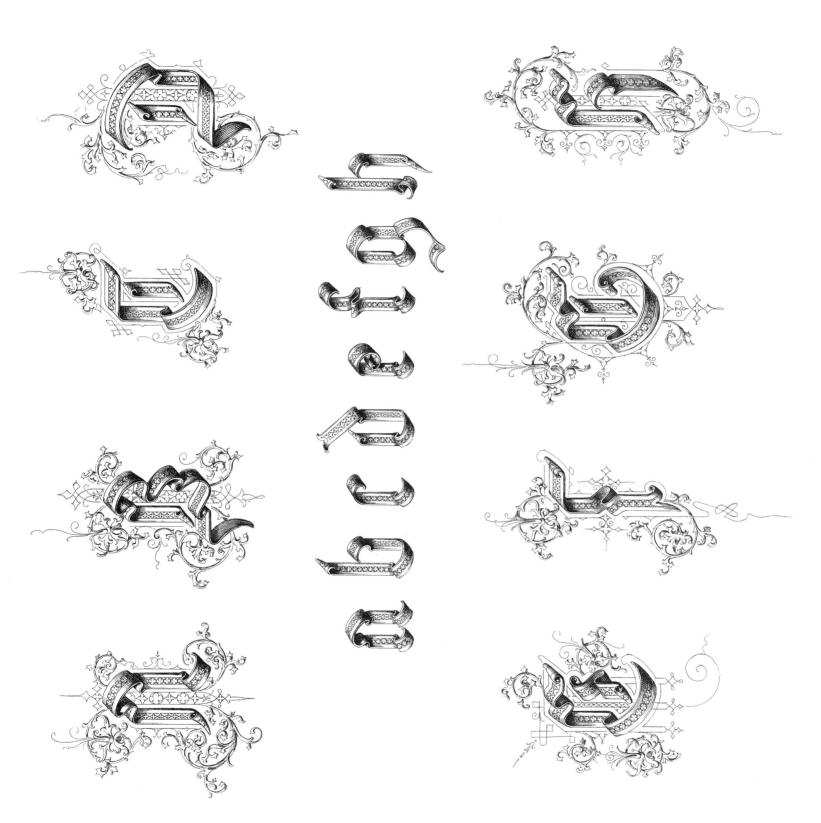

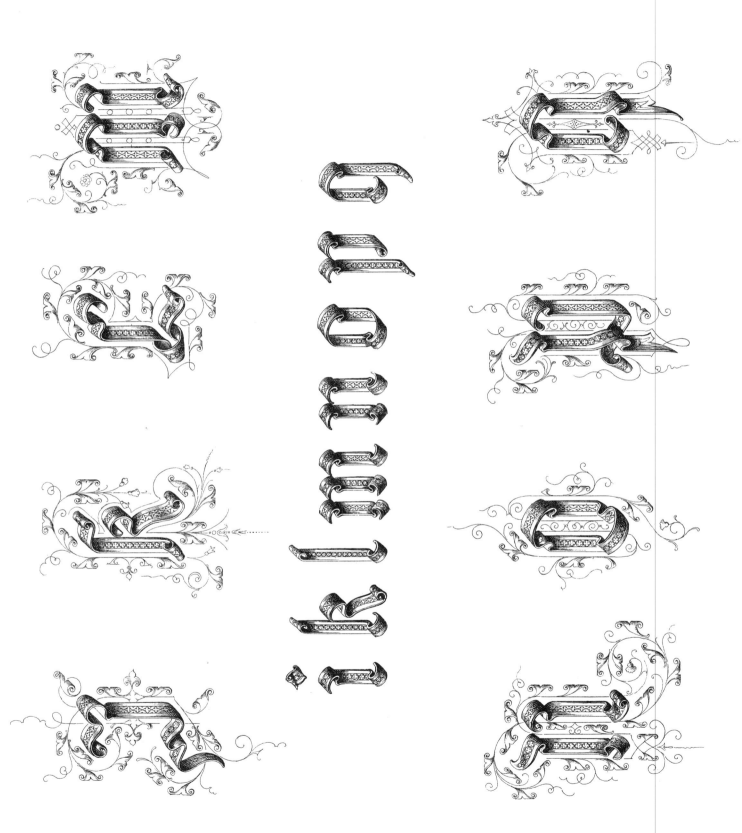

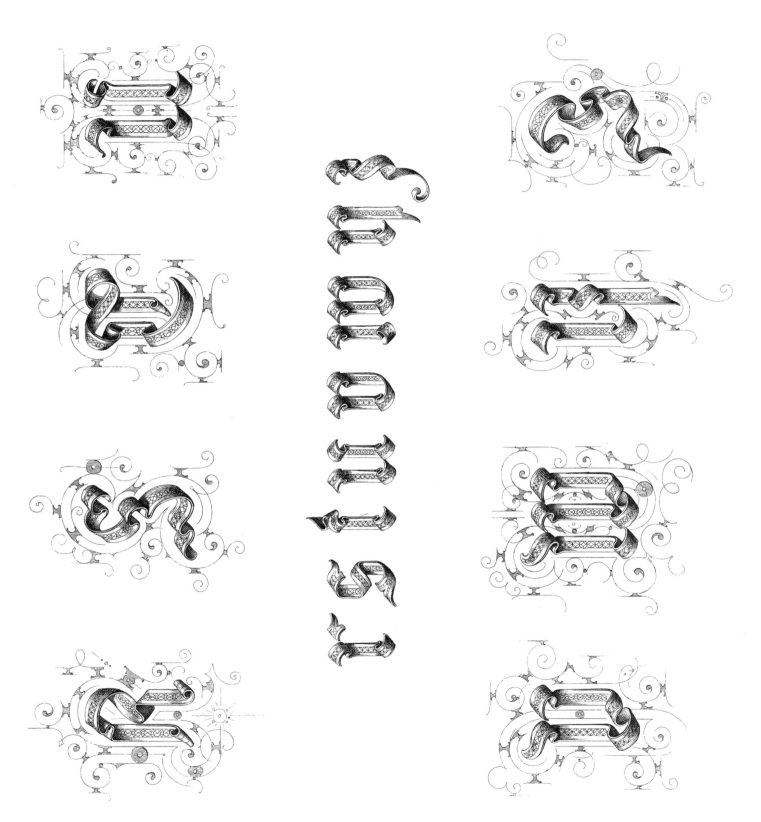

Klimsch

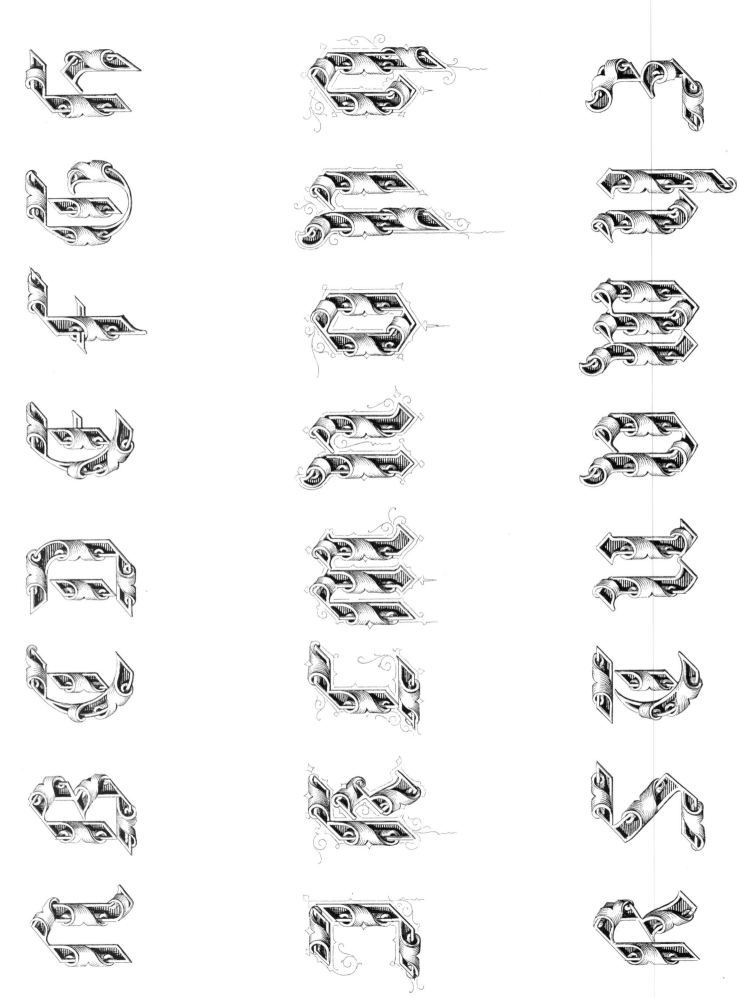

Klimsch

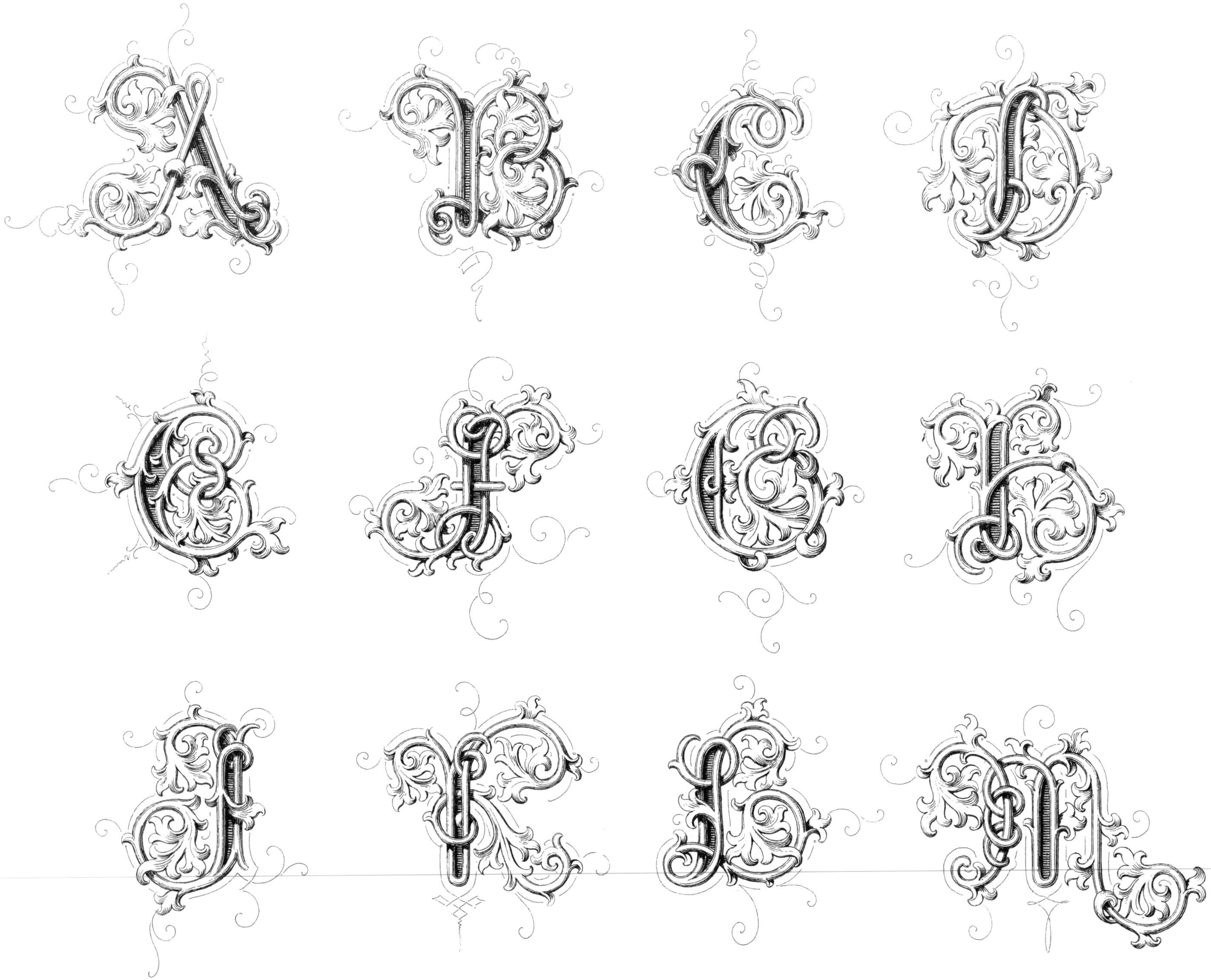

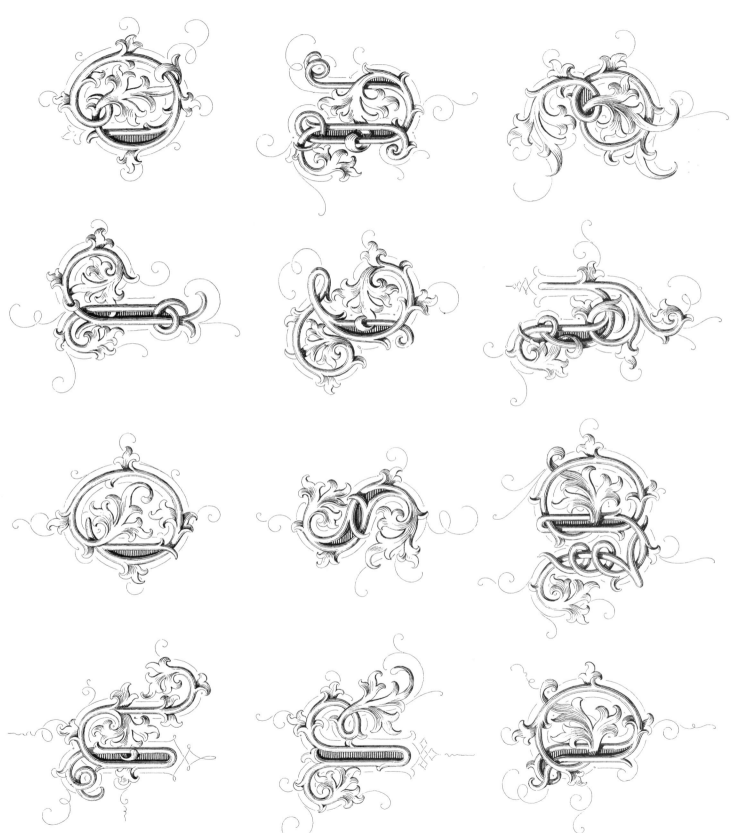